D0330265

MOVING VOICES

HANSIB PUBLICATIONS

MOVING VOICES

BLACK PERFORMANCE POETRY

ASHER & MARTIN HOYLES

HANSIB

First published in Great Britain in 2002
by Hansib Publications Limited
London: PO Box 34621, London E17 4GL
Hertfordshire: Orchard Road, Royston, Hertfordshire SG8 5HA

www.hansib-books.com

ISBN 1 870518 64 0

© Asher & Martin Hoyles (for text)

© Individual poets (for written & recorded poems)

All rights reserved. No part of this publication may be reproduced, stored in or introduced into
a retrieval system, or transmitted, in any form, or by any means, electronic, mechanical,
photocopying, recording or otherwise, without the prior written permission of the publisher.

Cover design by Graphic Resolutions, Hertfordshire, England

Production by Books of Colour, Hertfordshire, England

Printed and bound by Interprint Limited, Malta

ACKNOWLEDGEMENTS

We would like to thank all those who agreed to be interviewed for the book and also the following for their invaluable help and encouragement in producing it: Arif Ali and Kash Ali at Hansib Publications, Martin Brown at Waterhouse Studios, David Dabydeen, Gary Douglas, Janice Durham and Sarah White at New Beacon Bookshop, Margaret Hoyles, Graham Jeffery, Gary McLaren and Kevin Ramage at The Owl Bookshop, Victoria Mosley, John Parsons, Isha Persaud at Hansib Publications, Michael Rosen, John and Carol Smailes at Selecta Sound, Keith Wynn - Photocraft.

CREDITS

Edward Kamau Brathwaite by Julian Stapleton; Paul Robeson courtesy of *Daily World*; Sojourner Truth from National Portrait Gallery, Smithsonian Institute DC; Marcus Garvey from Astor, Lenox and Tilden Foundations; Louise Bennett from Sangster's; Paul Laurence Dunbar from General Collections, Library of Congress; Ma Rainey from New York Public Library Picture Collection; Maya Angelou by Susan Mullally Clark; Michael Smith by Julian Stapleton; Benjamin Zephaniah by Asher Hoyles; The Schooner *Flight* extract from 'Star-Apple Kingdom' from COLLECTED POEMS: 1948-1984 by Derek Walcott. Copyright 1986 by Derek Walcott. Reprinted by permission of Farrar, Straus and Giroux, LLC; Asher Hoyles from Black Sisters of Camden; Cuban Redd by Carol Bennett; Levi Tafari by John MacDonald; Michael Groce at Paradigm Club Nights, ICA, 2000, photo by Francine Lawrence.

Authors' Note: Every reasonable effort has been made to credit correctly. Any notified omissions will be corrected in future editions.

CONTENTS

Introduction

The Oral Tradition *9*
African Culture *13*
African Americans *21*
Caribbean Culture *34*
Oral Poetry *41*
Performance Poetry *51*
Black Performance Poetry in England *63*

The Poets

Benjamin Zephaniah *71*
Valerie Bloom *83*
John Lyons *95*
Asher Hoyles *109*
Adisa *123*
Cuban Redd *135*
Levi Tafari *147*
Patience Agbabi *163*
Michael Groce *175*
Cynthia Hamilton *187*
James Berry *199*
Jean 'Binta' Breeze *211*

Bibliography *223*

INTRODUCTION

In order to trace the origins of Black performance poetry in England, we need to look back to African culture. We have to see how that culture was carried to the New World by millions of slaves who survived the journey across the Atlantic, and how it adapted and grew despite attempts by the slave-owners to destroy it. Aspects of that culture were then brought again across the Atlantic to England where they have nurtured the poetry which we celebrate today as one of the most vibrant aspects of contemporary culture.

THE ORAL TRADITION

De way wi use de word
might come like a new fashion
I will tell yuh its an ancient tradition
Dat started out inna Africa
den reached de plantations of America
and moved across to de Caribbean
and now finds itself inna England
Suh wi just use dat tradition
fe express and explain fe wi situation
Suh don't think it was because of exploitation
it was intelligence and being one wid creation

Levi Tafari, *De WORD*, 1989

> dub poechree
> is ah paart ov
> de oral tradishan
> its chanted
> by de ooman
> and its chanted
> by de man
> ittah cum way back
> from innah Afrika lan
> if yuh tink ah any lie
> jus ask anyone
> who no
> bout de griot
> im will tell yuh
> bout fe wi histree

Moqapi Selassie, *Dub Poet Lekka Mi*

The oral tradition is a heritage of song, speech and performance visible in such folk forms as the litanic work songs, chants, battle songs, Queh Queh [wedding] songs, hymns, thousands of calypsos, mentos and reggae songs, sermons of both the grass-roots and establishment churches, riddles, jokes and word-games.

Gordon Rohlehr, *Voiceprint*, 1989

Once upon a time, all poetry was oral poetry. Before writing was invented - about 5,000 years ago - the only way to express poetic language was through the human voice. And human beings had been reciting and performing, singing and chanting in many voices for 100,000 years, beginning in Africa!

Even after writing had been invented, the ability to read and write was confined to only a few people. The majority continued to express and enjoy their verbal culture through oral communication.

In nineteenth-century Britain - the most advanced industrial country in the world - most citizens were illiterate. Only in the twentieth century was there at last a majority of people who could read and write.

In the rest of the world there are vast differences in the literacy rates between countries and within countries. The figures do not, however, always confirm what we might expect. Cuba and the south Indian state of Kerala, for example, both have higher literacy rates than the United States.

Since literature became established, there has usually been a close interplay between oral culture and written culture. Some of the most famous literary works in the world are based on oral tales. About 2,700 years ago, the earliest surviving Greek author, Homer, wrote down the *Iliad* and *Odyssey*, epic poems which were based on tales of the Trojan War, which had enjoyed a period of oral performance and composition before they were recorded in writing. Even religious texts often began as oral works: the early Christian gospels, the Qur'an, and the Hindu and Buddhist scriptures existed in oral form before being written down.

Over 1,000 years ago, the first written stories of *The Arabian Nights* (or *The Thousand and One Nights*), appeared, originating from oral tales from India, Persia and Arabia. They had circulated orally for centuries in the Arab world before they were collected and written down.

The story-teller, Shahrazad, who has to tell a tale every night to save herself from execution, is described in the Prologue as having "read the books of literature, philosophy and medicine. She knew poetry by heart, had studied historical reports, and was acquainted with the sayings of men and the maxims of sages and kings. She was intelligent, knowledgeable, wise and refined." In other words, she combined the skills of both literary and oral culture. Nevertheless, despite their immense popularity throughout the world, the tales were viewed with condescension and contempt by Arab men of letters of the eighteenth and nineteenth centuries.

Some of the most celebrated works of European literature have used the speech of the people, instead of the more difficult literary language, to convey their message. Dante wrote *The Divine Comedy* at the beginning of the fourteenth century in his local Italian dialect, rather than scholarly Latin, in order to appeal to the common reader, particularly women, who knew no Latin. As a consequence, his poetry was criticised for its "lowness, vulgarity, and lack of proper dignity".

Later in the same century, Chaucer's *Canterbury Tales* was largely derived from popular tales from all over Europe and the Orient, each ending with some proverbial wisdom. Chaucer often used colloquial language for his characters, and his use of popular English for his poetry, as opposed to aristocratic French or scholarly Latin, helped to establish English as the main language in the country.

In seventeenth-century Spain, Cervantes used folktales and proverbs in writing *Don Quixote*, and the character of Sancho Panza represents the speech of the common man. In the eighteenth century, Robert Burns, Scotland's most famous poet, wrote in his Ayrshire dialect and performed his poems in the capital city. As Paul Robeson observed: "Would Robert Burns have been as great a poet if he had denied his ploughman speech and aped the gentlemen of his day?"

William Blake wrote some of his poetry to be accessible to children and he used to sing his *Songs of Innocence and Experience* to small groups of friends. Turkey's most famous twentieth-century poet, Nâzim Hikmet, revolutionised Turkish poetry in the 1930s. He overturned Ottoman literary traditions by using the language of the people and writing in free verse.

There is a popular oral tradition of poetry in Pakistan, as Rukhsana Ahmad points out in *We Sinful Women*: "Poetry in Urdu is not the exclusive property of the cultural elite. Poetry readings, or *mushai'ras*, are an established and popular convention for Urdu speakers and attract many people who may not otherwise view themselves as 'literary' or who may not be in the habit of buying books. As some of this poetry is also set to music and sung, its use for political influence cannot be underestimated."

Periodically, when literature becomes too 'literary' and elitist, it needs to be opened up to popular culture, as can be seen in Shakespeare's plays which were watched by all sections of society. This process is also evident in the flowering at different times of working-class writing, women's writing and Black writing. In *Liberating Voices: Oral Tradition in African American Literature*, Gayl Jones, the African American poet and novelist, explains how something similar happened in Japanese literature: "In early Japan, prose was written in Chinese, the language of the Japanese court; to write in the Japanese vernacular was thought vulgar. Only women, untrained in Chinese, wrote novels in Japanese; thus the first intrusions of Japanese oral culture into the novel were made by women."

AFRICAN CULTURE

"Oral poetry and performance have been important features of South African society since the development of the first human communities on the subcontinent."

Duncan Brown, *Voicing the Text*, 1998

> There is a memory in the chant
> of the lyrics man, conjuring up
> that land we have all heard about
> and want to see across the sea.

Kwame Dawes, *Shook Foil*, 1997

"While the poetic political compositions of the great anti-imperialist Somali fighter, Hassan, will be known by heart by every Somali-speaking herdsman, not a line by even the best of African poets in foreign languages will be known by any peasant anywhere in Africa."

Ngugi Wa Thiong'o, *Decolonising the Mind: The Politics of Language*, 1986

Written history within Africa has been recorded in Arabic as far back as the thirteenth century. Despite European representation of Africans as uncivilised and illiterate, there have been literate peoples in Africa for centuries, for example, the Ethiopians in the north, the Zulus in the south, the Yorubas and Hausas in the west and the Swahili in the east. In sixteenth-century Timbuktu, for example, Ahmed Baba was the author of more than forty books.

Nevertheless, most verbal culture in Africa, as in the rest of the world, was expressed orally in more than a thousand different languages. All types of knowledge - religion, history, medicine, magic, astrology - would be transmitted by word of mouth. Paul Robeson

Timbuktu

observed that his ancestors in Africa considered sound to be particularly important, which was why they produced "great talkers, great orators, and, where writing was unknown, folktales and oral tradition kept the ears rather than the eyes sharpened". He added, "I am the same. I hear my way through the world."

Proverbs
The use of proverbs was one of the main ways of handing down the wisdom of generations. As a Sierra Leone proverb has it: "Proverbs are the daughters of experience." According to Jan Knappert in *The A-Z of African Proverbs*: "It is highly probable that the total number of proverbs circulating in the whole of Africa may surpass one million." Some of the knowledge people have may be lost when they die, as expressed in the proverb: "When an elder dies, it is as if a whole library had burned down."

The law in oral cultures can be enshrined in proverbs, as Walter Ong explains: "A judge in an oral culture is often called on to articulate sets of relevant proverbs out of which he can produce equitable decisions in the cases under formal litigation before him."

There is also a connection between proverbs and poetry, as Knappert points out: "Among the Swahili, the proverb-maker has to be a poet; his new proverb must have a rhythm and ideally a rhyme too. Thus many proverbs are fixed into one or two lines of very fine verse." Among the Akan of Ghana almost every proverb can also be reproduced on drums.

Story-telling

Another major aspect of African culture is story-telling. The stories would be handed down by mothers and grandmothers, often consisting of fables about intelligent animals who survive by their wits, for example, the wily weasel, Kabundi, the clever tortoise, Kobe, or the crafty hare, Sungura, from Tanzania. The most famous is the spider, Anancy, from West Africa (Ghana, Liberia, Sierra Leone), who, like the god Esu, was a trickster and incorrigible prankster, often causing havoc just for the fun of it.

The Kenyan writer, Ngugi Wa Thiong'o recalls his excitement at hearing these stories in his mother tongue and his disappointment when they were suppressed in his colonial school: "Orature (oral literature) in Kenyan languages stopped. In primary school I now read simplified Dickens and Stevenson alongside Rider Haggard. Jim Hawkins, Oliver Twist, Tom Brown - not Hare, Leopard and Lion - were now my daily companions in the world of imagination."

Ngugi was educated to write in English and published several books, but he realised that he was not reaching his own people. He decided to write in his native African language and his novel in Gikuyu, *Devil on the Cross*, became a popular success, with people reading it aloud in bars. In the same way, Indian writers who write in English cannot be understood by 95% of the people in the Indian subcontinent.

Story-telling is a performance art which relies on dramatic effect. It often involves improvisation, a highly valued skill in West African culture. As Geneva Smitherman explains in *Black Talk*, this relates to "the African concept of *Nommo*, the Word, which is believed to be the force of life itself. To speak is to make something come into being." The Senegalese singer, Youssou N'Dour, relates this story-telling to rap: "In the past we had something called *tassou*, where women rap about everyday things to African rhythms. Today in Senegal rappers talk about our traditions and our society."

Poetry

The main male orator in West African society was the griot, a combination of poet, musician and historian. He was known as 'Okeyame' in Ghana, 'Diali' in Mali, and 'Jali' in the Gambia. The griot acted as both history book and newspaper, with similarities to the European court jester or travelling troubadour. He could praise a ruler, but also be a social critic. He was a living archive of the people and he had hundreds of years of history committed to memory. His role was both spiritual and political, as a Gambian griot says: "We were the vehicle of government policy. We had in our charge the stores of high state secrets centuries old."

Many African societies allow poets an unusual freedom of speech to criticise those in power, but a major role for the poet in southern African society was that of the *imbongi*, or praise singer. He could sometimes compose and improvise his poetry for particular occasions, but among the Zulu, for instance, the praise poems of past chiefs were in fixed form and had to be learnt by heart. Nelson Mandela was the subject of praise poems at his inauguration as State President. Any person, however, can be praised in these poems, either for their skills or personality. Often the praise poems are performed at incredible speed, similar to contemporary rappers.

These were professional poets, but composing poetry could also be a general skill. Among the Akan of Ghana, for example, the women were responsible for intoning laments during public mourning. All Akan girls were expected to compose songs and perform them at relatives' funerals, though some women were considered particularly expert and would have larger repertoires than others.

In southern Africa, all Sotho boys had to be able to compose and perform praise poetry. After their initiation they had to recite their own praise poems in public. Likewise among some Zambian peoples a young man had to sing a song of his own composition at his marriage, while each woman had to have her own personal repertoire of songs to sing publicly as solos.

Drum Poetry

Drum poetry is widespread in the tropical forests of Africa. Because most African languages depend on the tone of the voice for meaning, these tones can be reproduced on a two- or three-toned drum, as can the rhythmic patterns of the language. Certain conventional drum phrases are used which have a poetic ring, different from everyday language. For instance, among the Kele people of the Congo, the phrase for 'rain' is "the bad spirit son of spitting cobra and sunshine"; for 'white man' it is either "red as copper, spirit from the forest" or "he enslaves the people, enslaves the people who remain in the land". When a message is sent in drum language, the tones of these phrases are understood by people many miles away in the forests.

West African drum poetry is performed at funerals, to praise rulers, to record history and to express proverbs. Among the Yoruba of Nigeria each of their many types of poetry can be recited on the drum, and the *oriki*, or praise poems, are drummed as often as they are sung.

In Ghana, the famous Akan talking drums are used to salute the chief and usher him to his seat:

> Chief, you are about to sit down,
> Sit down, great one.
> Sit down, gracious one.
> Chief, you have plenty of seating space.
> Like the great branch, you have spread all over this place.
> Let us crouch before him with swords of state.
> Ruler, the mention of whose name causes great stir,
> Chief, you are like the moon about to emerge.
> Noble ruler to whom we are indebted,
> You are like the moon:
> Your appearance disperses the famine.

Other instruments, too, are used to send verbal messages, such as whistles, horns, bells, gongs, stringed instruments and flutes.

Memory
Non-literate people attach great value to good memory. The Bushong people of the Congo, for example, can trace their oral history through the reign of their kings back to the thirteenth century. During the reign of their 98th king, Bo Kama Bomanchala, there was a total eclipse of the sun, which has been identified as 30 March 1680.

In *The Story of Africa* Basil Davidson describes travelling across the plains of the Sahel, south of the Sahara Desert, and meeting a teller of history: "I can recall an occasion when the teller, a woman, came into an inn on the trail to Ka Ba at sundown while we were resting, talking quietly, tired from the day's journey. There was a murmur of welcome, for tellers of history in these parts also sing ballads and songs of love and sorrow, comforters to the weary. Graceful in her long white gown, this singer had come to entertain as well as to instruct."

She sang in the Malinke language about the reign of Sundiata Keita who brought peace and honour to the land: "The tale is long and full of magic and marvels; and the memory is also long, for Sundiata ruled here 700 years ago. Other tales recall times still more remote, going back even to the *Kaya Magha*, the Lord of Gold who reigned over ancient Ghana before the Vikings found America or the Normans crossed to England."

Another example of the importance of memory within the African oral tradition is told by Jomo Kenyatta who became the first president of Kenya: "In 1921 Kenya nationalists, unable to read, would gather round a reader of Garvey's newspaper, the *Negro World*, and listen to an article two or three times. Then they would run various ways through the forest, carefully to repeat the whole, which they had memorised, to Africans hungry for some doctrine which lifted them from the servile consciousness in which Africans lived."

This memory was to be crucial to the Africans who were sold into slavery, as G. Llewellyn Watson points out in *Jamaican Sayings*: "Once again, we are reminded that the Africans who were carried away to the Americas did not carry books or parchments. But they succeeded in taking with them a great amount of knowledge, precisely because of the excellent development of their memory skills. In this way, not only mere recollections, but also typically African cultural traits are found in the tales, narratives and legends of the people of the diaspora in the Americas."

In *Folk Culture of the Slaves in Jamaica*, Edward Kamau Brathwaite makes the same point regarding their religion: "The slave ship became a kind of psycho-physical space capsule, carrying intact the carriers of the kind of invisible/atomic culture I have been describing; so that every African on those ships had within him/herself the potential of reconstruction; every mortal individual African (now slave), blessed

Edward Kamau Brathwaite

with religious gift, carried within himself the potential of explosion: the ability to use, starting with nothing more than his nakedness and breath, a whole wide range of remarkably complex resources."

He goes on to ask: "Could a captured, naked bishop have made/ survived that passage and with nothing other than his *breath*, rebuilt his church: texts, vestments, altar, aisle?"

The fact that most of the African slaves came from oral cultures is evident from the idea of the talking book which is employed by several ex-slave authors at the end of the eighteenth century. The first writer to use this metaphor was Gronniosaw in *A narrative of the most remarkable particulars in the life of James Albert Ukawsaw Gronniosaw, an African Prince*, published in 1770. He recalls hearing his master reading prayers to the ship's crew: "I was never so surprised in my life, as when I saw the book talk to my master, for I thought it did as I observed him to look upon it, and move his lips. I wished it would do so with me. As soon as my master had done reading, I followed him to the place where he put the book, being mightily delighted with it, and when nobody saw me, I opened it, and put my ear down close upon it, in great hopes that it would say something to me; but I was sorry, and greatly disappointed, when I found that it would not speak."

AFRICAN AMERICANS

"From the first African captives, through the years of slavery, and into the present century black Americans kept alive important strands of African consciousness and verbal art in their humor, songs, dance, speech, tales, games, folk beliefs, and aphorisms."

Lawrence W. Levine, *Black Culture and Black Consciousness*, 1977

"No one could wish for a more advantageous heritage than that bequeathed to the black writer in the South: a compassion for the earth, a trust in humanity beyond our knowledge of evil, and an abiding love of justice. We inherit a great responsibility as well, for we must give voice to centuries not only of silent bitterness and hate but also of neighbourly kindness and sustaining love."

Alice Walker, *The Black Writer and the Southern Experience*, 1970

"Any people who could endure all of that brutalization and keep together, who could undergo such dismemberment, resuscitate itself, and endure until it could take the initiative in achieving its own freedom is obviously more than the sum of its brutalization. Seen in this perspective, theirs has been one of the great human experiences and one of the great triumphs of the human spirit in modern times - in fact in the history of the world."

Ralph Ellison, *A Very Stern Discipline*, 1967

There are examples of slaves who were literate, such as the one observed by a European in 1773 who wrote out a line from the Qur'an. Most slaves, however, were not literate and there was a determined effort by slave-masters to keep them in that state. In 1739, the Stono Rebellion of slaves took place in South Carolina. Although barely a hundred people were involved, they marched to Georgia, "Dancing, Singing and Beating Drums". There they were attacked and most of them killed by the South Carolina militia. The state then enacted laws against both literacy and drumming, making it an offence to teach slaves to write and forbidding them to use or keep "drums, horns, or other loud instruments, which may call together or give sign or notice to one another of their wicked designs and purposes".

Other states also declared it illegal for slaves to be taught to read and write. In North Carolina, a free Negro caught teaching a slave to read was "fined, imprisoned, or whipped, at the discretion of the court, not exceeding thirty-nine lashes, nor less than twenty lashes".

As Frederick Douglass, the great anti-slavery campaigner, records: "It is almost an unpardonable offence to teach slaves to read in this Christian country." In his autobiography, published in 1845, he tells how, while still a slave, he learnt to read from little white boys he met in the street. He gave bread to "the hungry little urchins, who, in return, would give me that more valuable bread of knowledge".

Similarly, William Wells Brown, who wrote *The President's Daughter* (1853), the first novel in African American literature, describes how he learnt to read only after he had escaped from slavery. He persuaded two little boys to teach him to read by bribing them with barley sugar, and he learnt to write by chalking on fences: "All board fences within half a mile of where I lived were marked over with some kind of figures I had made, in trying to learn how to write."

So slaves were forbidden access to western literary culture and attempts were also made to destroy their own African oral culture. They were given new names, which was particularly traumatic, given the significance attached to people's names in West Africa. A name is often identified with a person's soul or the souls of ancestors and therefore seen as sacred. In Yoruba, a name can telescope a whole sentence or phrase describing the child and it often reflects much thought on the part of the child's parents.

Africans from the same region were often separated from each other to destroy their languages and prevent rebellion. Nevertheless, African languages were still spoken well into the nineteenth century, when the slave trade gradually ceased, and English took over.

In a similar way the colonial powers in Africa often tried to stop students speaking their own African languages. Ngugi Wa Thiong'o recalls this happening in his colonial school in Kenya: "One of the most humiliating experiences was to be caught speaking Gikuyu in the vicinity of the school. The culprit was given corporal punishment - three to five strokes of the cane on bare buttocks - or was made to carry a metal plate around the neck with inscriptions such as 'I AM STUPID' or 'I AM A DONKEY'."

In the United States, discouraging Black people from reading continued well into the twentieth century. The novelist, Richard Wright records in his autobiography, *Black Boy*, how, in the 1920s, he was not allowed to use the library in Memphis. He had to borrow a white man's card and pretend he was taking books out for him.

During the same period in the new state of Oklahoma, which had no tradition of slavery, Ralph Ellison records: "When I was a small child there was no library for Negroes in our city, and not until a Negro minister invaded the main library did we get one. For it was discovered that there was no law, only custom, which held that we could not use these public facilities."

As well as not being allowed access to literature, slaves were not always permitted to speak the same language as the slave-holders, as a freed slave explained soon after the American Civil War: "I was once whipped because I said to missis, 'My mother sent me'. We were not allowed to call our mammies 'mother'. It made it come too near the way of the white folks".

At the beginning of the nineteenth century, slaves were also discouraged from going to Christian revival meetings. David Walker, the free Black abolitionist and orator, wrote in his *Appeal*: "Christian Americans not only hinder the Africans, but thousands of them will absolutely beat a coloured person nearly to death, if they catch him on his knees, supplicating the throne of grace." Organised terror was used to prevent Black people from being Christians: hot coals were poured on the feet of slaves kneeling in prayer at revival meetings.

Retention Theory
In the first half of the twentieth century, most cultural theorists held the view that African culture in America had more or less been wiped out. One of the few exceptions was Paul Robeson, the great singer and political activist. He was also a scholar and a linguist who made a study of African languages. After researching Swahili and the Bantu group from the east coast of Africa, he wrote in 1934: "From them I passed on to the West Coast Negro languages and immediately found

Paul Robeson

a kinship of rhythm and intonation with the Negro-English dialect which I had heard spoken around me as a child. It was to me like a homecoming, and I felt that I had penetrated to the core of African culture when I began to study the legendary traditions, folksong and folklore of the West African Negro." The dances, songs and religion of the African American, he maintained, were the same as those of his "cousins" in Africa "whom he has never seen, of whose existence he is only dimly aware". He, himself, identified a number of Ibo words and phrases which had been passed down to him by members of his family.

In the second half of the twentieth century, since the Civil Rights Movement, retention theory, which looks at 'Africanisms' or 'survivals' from African culture, has been more and more dominant. As the Yoruba proverb from Nigeria states: "However far the stream flows, it never forgets its source."

One example of retention and development is 'the dozens', a rhyming game played mainly by teenage males, in which one opponent attacks another by reciting traditional insults directed at the other opponent's relatives, particularly his mother. The game is a test of keeping one's cool as well as a test of creative skills. It derives from the African tradition of institutional insults and ancestor derision.

Maya Angelou celebrates this activity in a poem called 'The Thirteens (Black)':

> Your Momma took to shouting,
> Your Poppa's gone to war,
> Your sister's in the streets,
> Your brother's in the bar,
> The thirteens. Right On.
>
> Your cousin's taking smack,
> Your uncle's in the joint,
> Your buddy's in the gutter,
> Shooting for his point,
> The thirteens. Right On.
>
> And you, you make me sorry,
> You out here by yourself,
> I'd call you something dirty,
> But there ain't nothing left,
> 'cept
> The thirteens. Right On.

The Norton Anthology of African American Literature, published in 1997, contains the following: "Many new black arrivals, whether coming in the seventeenth century, the eighteenth, or the nineteenth century, could immediately communicate together using a common creole language that had facilitated commerce back home in Africa. What is clearer than ever now is that the Africans also brought with them a vast storehouse of stories - along with other expressive forms as songs, dances, styles of worship, games, patterns of adornment, and the like that helped them to maintain on the new continent at least the broad outlines of their original world-view. Despite the ravages of the Middle Passage and the violence of slavery as an institution, one finds among African Americans story types, characters, motifs, and styles of telling that bear the distinctive traits of south Saharan Africa's ways of making stories."

Similarly, *The Oxford Companion to African American Literature*, which also came out in 1997, lists elements of folklore which had their origin in Africa: "The most renowned aspects of the African American oral tradition are folktales and folk music. Historically, African Americans have told a wide assortment of folktales, from tales of the sacred and the supernatural (creation legends, ghost stories, folk sermons, testimonials, and preacher tales) to secular tales (morality tales, trickster tales, and jokes)."

The Toast

One of these folktales is 'the toast', a dramatic traditional narrative performed in rhymed couplets, telling the story of badmen and outlaws, such as the notorious Black folk bandit, Stackolee. When sentenced to a ninety-nine year sentence, Stackolee boasts:

> Judge, ninety-nine ain't no god-damn time
> My father's in Sing Sing doing two ninety-nine.

Men who could recite such rhymes with flair earned a reputation as 'men of words'. This skill in 'toasting' is similar to that of rappers and DJs, who often use the rhythms and rhymes of oral poetry.

In William Wells Brown's *The President's Daughter*, Jack is asked by his master to give a toast on cotton and responds:

> The big bee flies high,
> The little bee makes the honey

> The black folks makes the cotton,
> And the white folks gets the money.

Muhammad Ali continued this tradition with his famous lines:

> Float like a butterfly
> Sting like a bee.

Oratory

We are familiar with the religious and political oratory of African Americans through the speeches of Martin Luther King, Jr and Malcolm X, but this is a practice that goes back for centuries.

In eighteenth-century Britain, Olaudah Equiano was one of many former slaves who toured the country addressing anti-slavery meetings. He had been kidnapped in Nigeria by slave-traders and, after a time in Virginia and the Caribbean, he finally saved up enough money to buy his freedom. Equiano then became the principal spokesman of Britain's Black community. His book, *The Interesting Narrative of the Life of Olaudah Equiano or Gustavus Vassa, the African*, contains extracts from his speeches.

In the nineteenth century, a whole host of slaves and former slaves became famous for their oratory, including Nat Turner, who led a slave revolt in Virginia and Denmark Vesey in South Carolina, Frederick Douglass, the greatest African American campaigner against slavery, and Sojourner Truth, who was illiterate but is remembered for her famous speech 'Ain't I a Woman?'.

When she was emancipated, Sojourner Truth decided to cast aside her slave name, Isabella, because she wanted to keep "nothin' of Egypt on me", as she said: "I went to the Lord an' asked him to give me a new name. And the Lord gave me Sojourner, because I was to travel up an' down the land, showin' the people their sins, an' bein' a sign unto them". She later asked for another name and "the Lord gave me Truth, because I was to declare the truth to the people".

Several of these anti-slavery campaigners came to Britain, including William and Ellen Craft, and William Wells Brown, who spent five years travelling around England, Ireland, Scotland and Wales speaking to audiences of thousands.

The great orator, Henry Highland Garnet also travelled all around

Sojourner Truth

Britain, as well as to France, Germany and Jamaica, before ending his days as Consul General in Liberia. In 1865, he became the first African American to deliver a sermon before the US House of Representatives. His grandfather was a slave who had been an African chieftain and warrior of the Mandingo people and when he was nine years old, Garnet himself escaped with his father from slavery in Maryland. He advocated

active resistance to slavery and at one meeting in England he sang
with feeling a slave song:

> See these poor souls from Africa
> Transported to America.
> We are stolen and sold to Georgia;
> Will you go along with me?
> We are stolen, and sold to Georgia;
> Come sound the jubilee!
>
> See the wives and husbands sold apart;
> Their children's screams will break any heart.
> There's a better day a-coming;
> Will you go along with me?
> Go sound the jubilee!

The most influential orator in the first half of the twentieth century
was Marcus Garvey, who illustrates the link between Africa, the US,
the Caribbean and Britain. He was born in Jamaica in 1887, but spent
most of his adult life in America where he built up the largest African
American mass movement in American history - the Universal Negro
Improvement Association. His 'Back to Africa' slogan was aimed at
restoring respect for African culture among Black Americans and, long
before the Civil Rights Movement, he said, "I shall teach the black
man to see beauty in himself". He spent the last five years of his life in
London where he used to speak in the open air at Hyde Park Corner.
Early in 1940, he suffered a stroke and died later that year.

It was as a teenager in Jamaica's capital, Kingston, that he first
learnt the skills of oratory. He was influenced by the speakers he heard
at barbershop forums and debates in local parks. He visited churches
and absorbed the oratorical style of a variety of preachers. He would
spend hours alone in his room reciting poetry and trying out different
gestures. He ended up lecturing in liberty halls throughout the United
States to audiences of tens of thousands of people, greeted by
tumultuous applause.

The continued importance of oration in African American culture
is stressed by the feminist writer, bell hooks. She knew as a child that
she wanted to be a writer, but it was the oral tradition which influenced

Marcus Garvey

her first, as she recalls in *Remembered Rapture* (1999): "Experiencing language as a transformative force was not an awareness that I arrived at through writing. I discovered it through performance - dramatically reciting poems or scenes from plays. At our all-black southern segregated schools the art of oration was deemed important. We were taught to perform. At school and at home we entertained one another with talent shows - singing, dancing, acting, reciting poetry."

In the same way, the African American writer Ralph Ellison records the oral tradition in Oklahoma: "But the places where a rich oral literature was truly functional were the churches, the schoolyards, the barbershops, the cotton-picking camps - places where folklore and gossip thrived. The drug store where I worked was such a place, where on days of bad weather the older men would sit with their pipes and tell tall tales, hunting yarns and homely versions of the classics. It was here that I heard stories of searching for buried treasure and of headless horsemen, which I was told were my father's versions told long before. There were even recitals of popular verse, 'The Shooting of Dan McGrew', and, along with these, stories of Jesse James, of Negro outlaws and black United States marshals, of slaves who became the chiefs of Indian tribes, and of the exploits of Negro cowboys."

Many people learnt their skill at oratory in church, and religion is another aspect of African culture which has survived and developed despite attempts to crush it. Many slave rebellions were actually planned in the church. There were strong links between Black Christianity and slave revolts, for example, in Barbados (1816), South Carolina (1822) and Jamaica (1831-32). In all of these uprisings there were powerful Christian leaders and networks of chapel membership which helped to organise the unrest. The religion was, however, a mixture of African and Christian, exemplified in America by the 'ring shout', a religious dance celebrating ancestors, derived from West Africa, in which the dancers shuffled in an anti-clockwise direction.

In *Black Talk*, Geneva Smitherman writes that the church has maintained the African concept of the unity of the sacred and the secular worlds: "The Black Church has been the single most significant force in nurturing the surviving African language and cultural traditions of African America. Over the centuries, the Church has stood as a rich reservoir of terms and expressions in Black lingo. Straight outa the Church have come expressions like 'on time', to acknowledge that something occurred at the appropriate psychological moment, and 'brotha/sista', as generic terms for any African American; proverbs such as 'God don't like ugly' and 'What go round come round'; and the ritual of 'shoutin' and 'gittin the spirit' when moved by the musical 'spirit' at soul concerts, clubs, cabarets, and other places of entertainment. In the spirit-getting, tongue-speaking, vision-receiving, Amen-saying, sing-song preaching, holy-dancing Traditional Black Church, the Oral Tradition is live!"

Music and Song

In Africa, men and women sang as they worked, and this practice continued among the slaves, as Samuel A. Floyd, in *The Power of Black Music*, explains: "While singing songs to accompany their digging, cutting, pulling, and driving, their basket weaving and grain grinding, these African Americans were constantly poking fun at themselves, their overseers, their masters, and visiting observers. Their humor was their armament in a culture in which they had little control". The slave masters realised that their slaves worked harder when they sang and that there was usually a lead singer who set the pace. When slaves were auctioned, singers with the strongest voices fetched the highest prices.

Floyd goes on to argue that "African musical traits and cultural practices not only survived but played a major role in the development and elaboration of African-American music." He lists some of the musical instruments of African origin, "banjo, musical saw, reed flutes, drums (where they were not prohibited), sticks or bones, and rattles of various kinds."

W.E.B. Du Bois provides an example of how African lullabies survived through the centuries of slavery. His grandfather's grandmother, seized by a Dutch trader around 1700, was brought to New England as a slave. The melody she crooned to her child was the same one sung to Du Bois by his mother. As he writes: "For two hundred years it has travelled down to us and we sing it to our children, knowing as little as our fathers what its words mean, but knowing well the meaning of its music."

The African musical tradition was to be crucial in the development of jazz, as Marshall Stearns points out in *The Story of Jazz*: "The continued existence of the ring-shout is of critical importance to jazz, because it means that an assortment of West African musical characteristics are preserved, more or less intact, in the United States - from rhythm and blues tonality, through the falsetto break and the call-and-response pattern, to the songs of allusion and even the motions of African dance."

African influences can also be observed in white culture. The banjo, for example, was taken up by white Americans particularly in the Appalachian mountains, leading John Edward Philips, in *Africanisms in American Culture*, to claim that "surviving styles of Appalachian banjo music are likely the most authentically African music in the United States". He also points to African influences on southern white cooking, religion, cowboy culture and language. In the same book Joseph E. Holloway lists many words that can be traced back to Wolof, the language of Senegal and the Gambia, for example, 'OK', 'bogus', 'phoney', 'guy', 'honkie' and 'hippie'.

Likewise, in poetry, when Ralph Ellison first read T. S. Eliot's *The Waste Land* (1922), he could see the "relationship between modern poetry and jazz music" and was fascinated by the poem's musicality: "Somehow its rhythms were often closer to those of jazz than were those of the Negro poets, and even though I could not understand then, its range of allusion was as mixed and as varied as that of Louis Armstrong". In the same way, Kamau Brathwaite has noted that T.S. Eliot's voice recordings influenced a generation of West Indian poets who were trying to use their own speech in their poetry.

CARIBBEAN CULTURE

"Any speech is as interesting as the people who speak it: it is the most revealing reflection of their lives. In Jamaica it has grown and flourished by preserving things from the past; by developing new and often surprising, amusing and imaginative meanings; by making a variety of new permutations and combinations, lively, penetrating and often remarkably apt. It has a character all its own of which none but the least imaginative can remain unaware."

Frederic G. Cassidy, *Jamaica Talk*, 1961

"We had brought ourselves. We had not come from nothing."

C. L. R. James, *The Making of the Caribbean People*, 1966

"Our people have preserved our heritage through music and the most searing of poetic insights, whether through song-lyrics and dub, Louise Bennett or Paul Keen-Douglas, in an attempt to ambush the society into self-healing and self-examination."

Rex Nettleford, *Inward Stretch Outward Reach: A Voice from the Caribbean*, 1993

There were differences between Caribbean and North American slave cultures, but also strong similarities, based on their African roots, as the social historian James Walvin writes in *Black Ivory*: "Jamaican slaves were quite different from those in Virginia, but the broader patterns of social life reveal remarkable similarities".

There has also been a similarity in the way their culture has been viewed. Following a series of strikes and demonstrations throughout the West Indies in the 1930s, a Royal Commission was sent out by the Colonial Office in 1938 to inquire into the state of the islands. The resulting Moyne Report contained the following: "Negroes were taken from lands where they lived no doubt in a primitive state. Their transfer to the West Indies unlike most other large-scale movements of population, did not involve the transfer of any important traces of their traditions and customs, but rather their almost complete destruction."

C.L.R. James's response to this is scathing: "Now it is impossible to produce a sentence that contains more mistakes and more gross misunderstandings and misrepresentations. The Negroes who came from Africa brought themselves. The report says that they left everything behind. But the Africans themselves are the most important and most valuable representatives of their civilisation. That when they came here they brought themselves, something of primary importance, never seems to come to the mind of all these people who write reports."

Music and Song

With themselves they brought their oral culture and their skills. Walvin describes similar accounts of music, song and dance throughout slave communities, all derived from African culture. When Monk Lewis, for example, visited his estates in Jamaica in 1816, he was everywhere greeted by singing and dancing: "Their music consisted of nothing but Gambys [drums], shaky-shekies, and kitty-katties; the latter is nothing but a flat piece of board with two sticks, the former is a bladder with a parcel of pebbles in it. But the principal part of the music to which they dance is vocal; one girl generally singing two lines by herself, and being answered by the chorus."

The singing and chorus is usually referred to as 'call and response' and in Africa these songs were usually sung by women. Call and response is a feature of work songs, folk songs and poetry. It is also evident in the way the congregation responds to the minister in church. This is derived from African religious practice. In Ghana, for example, Akan prayers would receive the response "Ampara ara" (It is just the truth) or "Yonn" (Yes, indeed!). A Jamaican example, recorded in 1843, refers to the potency of the Spanish drink, sangria, a mixture of wine and fruit juice:

> Sangaree kill de captain,
>   O dear, he must die;
> New rum kill de sailor,
>   O dear, he must die;
> Hard work kill de neger,
>   O dear, he must die.

A Caribbean work song of the same period has a similar refrain:

> If me want for go in a Ebo,
> Me can't go there!
> Since dem tief me from a Guinea,
> Me can't go there!
>
> If me want for go in a Congo,
> Me can't go there!
> Since dem tief me from my tatta [father],
> Me can't go there!
>
> If me want for go in a Kingston,
> Me can't go there!
> Since massa go in a England,
> Me can't go there!

As in America, Caribbean musical instruments developed from African ones, and the slave owners perceived a similar threat from some of them. In the eighteenth century, it became unlawful for "Slaves to assemble together, and beat their Military Drums, empty casks, and great Gourds, or blow their Horns or Shells". The reason was the same, that rebellions had often been planned at "Dances and Nightly Meetings of Slaves from different Plantations".

In the 1880s, the colonial government in Trinidad banned drum processions because of its worries about troubles at carnival time. Similarly, in St Lucia, there was a law forbidding the beating of a drum after 10 o'clock at night, within a mile of any town or village, which lasted well into the twentieth century.

One place drumming was allowed, however, was on warships. At the beginning of the nineteenth century, almost a fifth of American seamen were Black and there was a similar number of Black sailors in the British navy. As well as working alongside white seamen, they often had specialist roles such as cooks, interpreters or musicians who entertained the crew, like Joseph Emidy who played the violin and eventually settled in Cornwall. They were also employed as drummers to send instructions around the ship, especially in battle.

A crucial way of spreading ideas and culture was by way of these ships which were ploughing back and forth across the oceans of the world. It is interesting to note that seamen wrote the first six Black autobiographies published in English before 1800.

Folk Tales and Proverbs

African folk tales were also similar across the New World - Brer Rabbit stories in North America, Anancy stories in the Caribbean. 'Ananse' is the word for spider in Twi, one of the main languages of West Africa, and the spider is the chief character in the folk tales of the Ashanti people. Anancy is a trickster who survives by guile and cunning, a metaphor for the slave.

Writing of Antigua in 1844, Mrs Lanigan reports: "After dancing, I think the next favourite pastime of the negroes, particularly among the younger ones, is to collect together upon a fine moonlight night, and talk 'Nancy stories'. The far-famed 'Scheherezade' of the 'Arabian Nights' could scarcely invent more marvellous ones."

In Dominica, with its additional French influence, the storytellers were called *raconteurs*. They would tell traditional folk tales, called *contes*, which included rhymes, riddles, music, audience response and sometimes dancing.

Anancy stories are particularly popular in Jamaica where Louise Bennett collected and performed them. Many of them contain verses which are usually sung by the various animals in the tales and "these have been the true lullabies to Jamaican children for generations". She goes on to say: "Anancy, the trickify little spider man who speaks with a lisp and lives by his wits, is both comic and sinister, both hero and villain of Jamaican folk stories. He points up human weaknesses and shows how easily we can be injured and destroyed by our greed, or stupidity, or by confidence in the wrong people and things. He can change himself into whatever and whoever he wishes at certain times, and his stories make it quite plain that he is able to get away with tricks which ordinary mortals can't. He is a rascal but lovable, and every existing custom is said to have been started by Anancy: 'Is Anancy meck it.'"

As well as being an authority on Anancy stories, Louise Bennett also uses popular proverbs in her poetry. 'Dutty Tough' (The Ground is Hard), begins:

Louise Bennett

> Sun a-shine but tings noh bright,
> Doah pot a-bwile, bickle [food] noh nuff,
> River flood but water scarce yaw,
> Rain a-fall but dutty tuff!

Bob Marley draws on the same sources in his song 'Them Belly Full':

> Them belly full but we're hungry,
> A hungry man is an angry man,
> The rain a-fall but the dutty tuff,
> A pot a-cook but the food noh nuff.

Many Caribbean proverbs derive from Africa. For instance, the Jamaican proverb, "Rain never fall a one man door", or Bob Marley's lyric, "When the rain fall, it don't fall on one man's house", mirrors the Nigerian Yoruba and Cameroon Nyang proverb:

> The rain does not recognise anyone as friend
> Whomsover it sees it drenches.

Similarly, the Ashanti, "Wood already touched with fire is not hard to set alight" produces the Jamaican, "Ole fire stick no hard fe ketch"; and the Jamaican, "Sheep and goat no all one" reflects the Ashanti, "A sheep does not give birth to a goat".

Language

Caribbean creole or patois has developed from African and European languages and goes back to the beginnings of trade between Europe and West Africa. It developed also as a language that slaves could use without their masters understanding what they were saying. Caribbean English still retains strong African influences in its grammar and intonation. In Trinidad, for example, both French and English creole flourished, each influenced by Yoruba and by French and then English, as the island passed from one European power to the other.

In Jamaica, about ninety percent of patois is of English origin, with most of the rest being African, though there are also words from Arawak, Spanish, Portuguese, French, Chinese and Indian. Over 400 words derive from African languages. For example 'duppy', meaning ghost or spirit, comes from a Bantu language called Bube; 'obeah', the belief in spirits and spells, is from Twi, as is 'su-su', to gossip; 'nyam', meaning to eat, is common to a number of African languages.

For a long time, Caribbean English was looked down on as inferior, particularly in the education system, both in the West Indies and in England. Until fairly recently, Caribbean education was colonial, relying on text-books like Nelson's *West Indian Readers*, with their imperial message, to impart English culture. In *Voices of the Crossing*, James Berry recalls his experience at a Church of England elementary school in 1930s rural Jamaica: "A boy would be reprimanded or caned if a teacher caught him singing a Caribbean calypso. The acceptable would have been the singing of a song like *Drink to Me Only with thine Eyes* based on Ben Jonson's poem, or to be heard memorising a poem like *The Wreck of the Hesperus*."

The same point is made by Philip Sherlock, who was Vice-Chancellor of the University of the West Indies, in John Figueroa's *Caribbean Voices*. He writes in the foreword that he was brought up on Tennyson, Browning, Wordsworth, Keats and Shelley: "I belonged to a people without a literature. There was beauty; my island, like Prospero's, was full of sweet sounds; but why were there no voices?"

Likewise, in England, children with Caribbean backgrounds have often suffered low expectations, ridicule and discrimination because of their language. One of the ways that this has all been challenged is through poetry, as in Benjamin Zephaniah's 'Lesson Number Wan':

> Slavery waz wan day old,
> Me English lesson began,
> I survived de Atlantic crossing
> I survived shackles, de whip
> De immigration trick,
> Emerging 400 years later
> Wid me English in Black.
>
> When ordered to sing I rap
> When ordered to speak I chat
> When ordered to die I lived
> An I don't play cricket.

ORAL POETRY

"The resistance of literary studies to oral challenge is ironic in view of the debt of almost all poetic forms to oral rhythms and vocalizations, and the vital and continuing existence of oral genres worldwide."

Duncan Brown, *Voicing the Text*, 1998

> **Give me a word**
> **any word**
> **let it roll across your tongue**
> **like a dolly mixture.**
> **Open your lips**
> **say it loud**
> **let each syllable vibrate**
> **like a transistor.**

Patience Agbabi, *Prologue*, 2000

"In the end, it is through the oral poets that the Caribbean identity can be explored and celebrated in all its particularity."

Paula Burnett, *Caribbean Verse in English*, 1986

Oral poetry is poetry which calls out to be heard. It is based on the spoken word, the vernacular, the speech of the people.

As we have seen, oral culture had crossed the Atlantic with the African slaves and it became even more important as the slaves were denied access to literacy. Even when slavery was abolished, the oral tradition continued hand-in-hand with a growing literary tradition. At the end of the nineteenth century, several African American poets, such as James Campbell and the popular orator Daniel Webster Davis, performed their dialect poetry to Black audiences across America.

The most famous was Paul Laurence Dunbar (1872-1906) whose dialect verse was internationally admired. He performed his poems

throughout the US and went on a poetry-reading tour of England in
1897. From one of his poems comes the line "I know why the caged
bird sings", which was to become the title of Maya Angelou's first
volume of autobiography. His poem, 'An Ante-Bellum Sermon' is a
biblical call for freedom, cleverly combining politics and religion.
The last verse, ironically, changes tack in the last line to disarm the
criticism that the poet is being too political:

> But when Moses wif his powah,
>   Comes an' sets us chillen free,
> We will praise de gracious Mastah
>   Dat has gin us liberty;
> An' we'll shout ouah halleluyahs,
>   On dat mighty reck'nin' day,
> When we'se reco'nized ez citiz' -
> Huh uh! Chillen let us pray!

This combination of oral and literary culture was further developed in
the first decades of the twentieth century by poets of the Harlem
Renaissance who were profoundly interested in African American folk
culture. Some of the most famous, who explored the resources of the
blues, spirituals, proverbs, tales and sayings, were James Weldon
Johnson (1871-1938), Langston Hughes (1902-1967) and Sterling A.
Brown (1901-1989).

One of Johnson's poems, 'Lift Every Voice and Sing', written in
1900, was set to music by his brother and sung by Paul Robeson. It
later became known as the 'Negro National Anthem'. In the same
year, he wrote the dialect poem 'Sence You Went Away':

> Seems lak to me de stars don't shine so bright,
> Seems lak to me de sun done loss his light,
> Seems lak to me der's nothin' goin' right,
>   Sence you went away.
>
> Seems lak to me de sky ain't half so blue,
> Seems lak to me dat eve'ything wants you,
> Seems lak to me I don't know what to do,
>   Sence you went away.

Paul Laurence Dunbar

Seems lak to me dat eve'ything is wrong,
Seems lak to me de day's jes twice ez long,
Seems lak to me de bird's forgot his song,
        Sence you went away.

Seems lak to me I jes can't he'p but sigh,
Seems lak to me ma th'oat keeps gittin' dry,
Seems lak to me a tear stays in ma eye,
        Sence you went away.

Langston Hughes called himself a folk poet and used the resources of jazz, the blues and speech to write his poetry. His first collection of poetry, published in 1926, was called *The Weary Blues*. He later became known as 'The Poet Laureate of the Negro Race'. His poem 'Mother to Son' was written in 1922:

Well, son, I'll tell you:
Life for me ain't been no crystal stair.
It's had tacks in it,
And splinters,
And boards torn up,
And places with no carpet on the floor -
Bare.
But all the time
I'se been a-climbin' on,
And reachin' landin's,
And turnin' corners,
And sometimes goin' in the dark
Where there ain't been no light.
So boy, don't you turn back.
Don't you set down on the steps
'Cause you finds it's kinder hard.
Don't you fall now -
For I'se still goin', honey,
I'se still climbin',
And life for me ain't been no crystal stair.

Sterling A. Brown had a Master's Degree from Harvard University, but maintained throughout his life that his best teachers were the poor Black folk of the South. He wrote about African American art and folklore and his poetry was influenced by ballad and blues forms, by spirituals and work songs. 'Southern Road', for example, is a chain gang song which ends:

> White man tells me - hunh -
> Damn yo' soul;
> White man tells me - hunh -
> Damn yo' soul;
> Got no need, bebby,
> To be tole.
>
> Chain gang nevah - hunh -
> Let me go;
> Chain gang nevah - hunh -
> Let me go;
> Po' los' boy, bebby,
> Evahmo'....

Brown's tribute to Ma Rainey, the famous blues singer, contains this verse:

> O Ma Rainey,
> Sing yo' song;
> Now you's back
> Whah you belong,
> Git way inside us,
> Keep us strong....
> O Ma Rainey,
> Li'l an' low;
> Sing us 'bout de hard luck
> Roun' our do';
> Sing us 'bout de lonesome road
> We mus' go....

Ma Rainey

Una Marson

In *The Penguin Book of Caribbean Verse in English*, Paula Burnett calls Una Marson (1905-1965) "the Caribbean's first woman poet of note". Born in rural Jamaica, she came to England in 1932 where she became a political activist and feminist. In 1941, she was appointed full-time programme assistant at the BBC, organising broadcasts under the title 'Calling the West Indies'.

In 1943, she devised another programme called 'Caribbean Voices', which ran for fifteen years, in which she broadcast some of her own poems in her strong Jamaican accent . According to Edward Kamau Brathwaite, the programme was "the single most important literary catalyst for Caribbean creative and critical writing in English".

The title of John Figueroa's anthology of West Indian poetry was based on this programme. Many of the poems he included in the first volume in 1966 were obtained from the BBC archives and had not previously been available in print. Figueroa states that for many years the programme, 'Caribbean Voices', was "the main opportunity for any kind of publication by West Indian writers". There was, however, still prejudice against Caribbean accents. Figueroa recalls how even some Jamaicans thought his reading voice did not sound sufficiently 'English'.

Although Paula Burnett places Una Marson in the literary tradition, many of her poems clearly belong to the oral tradition, and this illustrates the fact that many poets switch between the two and that these traditions form a spectrum, rather than a split. Each tradition can influence the other. As Fred D'Aguiar writes in *Black British Poetry* (1988): "Although some poets are best heard in performance rather than read solely on the page, I would be hard-pressed to confine a poet to one realm or the other. At the level of composition many poets are moving towards a coalition of the two: the performance poem which also works on the page."

Marson's poetry was influenced by Langston Hughes and also by James Weldon Johnson, with whom she was in regular correspondence. She idolised the blues singer Bessie Smith, as can be seen in these verses from 'Brown Baby Blues':

> I got a brown baby
> Sweet as she can be

Una Marson

I got a brown baby
Sweet as she can be
But she ain't got no papa
Cause he's gone to sea

I love me baby
But she don't got no name
I love me baby
She don't got no name
Well wha' fe do
Dat is not her shame.

She was also influenced by her Baptist upbringing, as is evident in the call and response preaching of 'Gettin de Spirit':

Lord gie you chile de spirit
Let her shout
Lord gie you chile de power
An let her pray -
Hallelujah - Amen -
Shout sister - shout -
God is sen you His spirit
Shout - sister - shout

Shout sister - shout -
Hallelujah - Amen.
Can't you feel de spirit
Shout sister - shout
Hallelujah - Amen

Join de chorus,
We feel it flowing o'er us -
You is no chile of satan
So get de spirit
And shout - sister - shout -
Hallelujah - Amen -
Shout - sister - Shout!

One of her political poems, reminiscent of William Blake's 'Little Black Boy', is called 'Politeness':

> They tell us
> That our skin is black
> But our hearts are white.
>
> We tell them
> That their skin is white
> But their hearts are black.

In her autobiography of Una Marson, Delia Jarrett-Macauley writes: "By the early 1980s Una Marson's name had emerged as *the* pioneering African-Caribbean woman poet, the foremother of contemporary black women writers in Britain. Only the canon and the curse of literary history that has concealed women writers of one generation from the next had separated Una from her African-Caribbean daughters."

PERFORMANCE POETRY

"A piece of oral literature, to reach its full actualisation, *must be performed*. The text alone cannot constitute the oral poem. This *performance* aspect of oral poetry is sometimes forgotten, even though it lies at the heart of the whole concept of oral literature."

Ruth Finnegan, *Oral Poetry*, 1992

> Intellectuals an sociologists mus come an see
> What is happening now orally,
> It is really meking history bringing poetry alive
> To a dub or funky reggae, to jazz music, rock an jive.

Benjamin Zephaniah, *Rapid Rapping*, 1992

"I have been set apart by other creative writers a long time ago because of the language I speak and work in. From the beginning nobody ever recognised me as a writer. 'Well, she is doing dialect'; it wasn't even writing you know. Up to now a lot of people don't even think I write. They say 'Oh, you just stand up and say these things!'"

Louise Bennett, *Interview*, 1968

Performance poetry not only needs to be heard, it usually also has to be seen to be properly understood. It relies on rhythm, intonation, gesture, and sometimes music and song, to gain its effect. Mervyn Morris, the Jamaican poet and critic who is often credited with coining the phrase 'performance poetry', writes that the performance poem is "dependent for its meanings on the variable interaction between text, performer, audience and occasion".

Because it is not primarily written to be read, performance poetry has sometimes been criticised for not being properly 'crafted'. In an interview in 1973, Derek Walcott, for example, said that in writing "immediate poetry" the poet does not listen to his "inner ear". He criticised easily communicable theatre which "leaves out the most exciting part of poetry, which is its craft". Gordon Rohlehr responded in his introduction to *Voiceprint* that Walcott "fails to recognize that a poetry based on the oral tradition would require, seek and create its own crafting".

The performance poet's craft is in designing the poem for the stage. This demands just as much skill and often means revision and improvement after initial performances. The poems on the CD accompanying this book are sometimes slightly different from the written versions, illustrating the way in which they can change over time with performance. These poets really need a live audience to provide response and feedback. Unlike actors, performance poets are speaking their own lines. Unlike poets on the page, they face their audience directly. As Benjamin Zephaniah puts it in *Rapid Rapping*:

> So dey picking up de microphone fe dere expression
> Dey hav fe get it right or dey get verbal reaction.

There has been a revival of African American performance poetry since the 1970s, drawing on Black music and Black speech, blues and jazz, call and response, rap and improvisation. One of the most famous poets is Maya Angelou who performed one of her poems at the inauguration of President Clinton. Her poem 'Still I Rise' needs to be heard *and* seen, as she finishes it with her arm raised, pointing to the sky, improvising a further line "There I go!". The poem concludes:

> Out of the huts of history's shame
> I rise
> Up from the past that's rooted in pain
> I rise
> I'm a black ocean, leaping and wide,
> Welling and swelling I bear in the tide.
> Leaving behind nights of terror and fear
> I rise
> Into daybreak that's wondrously clear
> I rise
> Bringing the gifts that my ancestors gave,

Maya Angelou

> I am the dream and the hope of the slave.
> I rise
> I rise
> I rise.

Maya Angelou also tried her hand at writing a work song, but was disappointed with her first effort as it followed the tradition of male work songs. Eventually, she wrote a female work song called 'Woman Work', which begins:

> I've got the children to tend
> The clothes to mend
> The floor to mop
> The food to shop
> Then the chicken to fry
> The baby to dry
> I got company to feed
> The garden to weed
> I've got the shirts to press
> The tots to dress
> The cane to cut
> I gotta clean up this hut
> Then see about the sick
> And the cotton to pick.
>
> Shine on me, sunshine
> Rain on me, rain
> Fall softly, dewdrops
> And cool my brow again.

Louise Bennett

Like Una Marson, Louise Bennett also worked for the West Indies section of the BBC. It is remarkable that these two Jamaican voices were heard broadcasting from the home of standard English, decades before the BBC really accepted regional accents or dialect on its airwaves.

E. A. Markham writes of Louise Bennett in *Hinterland: Caribbean Poetry from the West Indies and Britain*: "She is the pioneering figure of the century in the oral tradition of Caribbean poetry, but while her work has always enjoyed great popularity with the public, she had to wait until vernacular poetry was accepted as 'literature' in the 1960s before she was recognised as a great Caribbean writer."

This indicates how powerful the prejudice and discrimination against oral poetry has been. Una Marson's dialect poetry was criticised as "ludicrous" and "farcical", written in a "broken language"; just as Langston Hughes's poetry about working class Black culture had been called "trash", reeking of "the gutter and the sewer".

Louise Bennett was born in 1919 in Kingston and began writing and performing poems as a teenager. Far from just standing up and saying things, her poetry is the result of detailed research and observation. She devoted her life to the study of Jamaican folklore, visiting the Maroons, attending old-time tea-meetings, religious ceremonies, dinkies (wakes), weddings and concerts throughout Jamaica. She became a leading folklore specialist, helping to save much of Jamaican folk material from extinction, for instance, by publishing collections of Anancy stories.

She was educated at St Simon's College and Excelsior College before moving to London in 1945 to study at RADA (Royal Academy of Dramatic Art). In England, she worked for repertory companies in Coventry, Huddersfield and Amersham. In 1955, she returned to Jamaica where she lectured in drama and Jamaican folklore at the University of the West Indies.

Louise Bennett acts in the role of social commentator through her poetry. She speaks about everyday life in Kingston, about the Second World War, politics, language, love and religion - all with a sense of humour and irony. For instance, when Jamaica became independent in 1962, she wrote:

> Independance wid a vengeance!
> Independance raisin' cain!
> Jamaica start grow beard, ah hope
> We chin can stan' de strain!

As Rex Nettleford writes, in the introduction to *Jamaica Labrish*, she is "a performer, accomplished and unrivalled". He goes on: "She stands firmly in a tradition of the spoken word, living as she does in a society in which anything worth knowing by a great many people has for a

Louise Bennett

long time been *told* and not written. The parson's pulpit and the politician's platform have supported our oracles throughout our history."

Since about 1936, she performed her work in crowded village halls across the island, but only some years later did she finally get some of her poems accepted by the *Sunday Gleaner*, the main Jamaican newspaper. Even these poems would often be read aloud, following the custom of a person reading the newspaper out loud to a small group of friends gathered in a country yard or in a barber shop. In the same way, in nineteenth-century England, newspapers were often read aloud for illiterate people to hear.

By 1962, when she had already published nine books, she still did not appear among the poets in the *Independence Anthology of Jamaican Poetry*, but was put at the back under 'Miscellaneous'! Her response to this treatment of dialect poetry had already been written way back in 1944 in 'Bans O' Killing'. In this poem she argues with Charlie that if he wants to destroy the Jamaican dialect of English, then he will logically have to kill off all the other English dialects which have produced some of the greatest poetry in the world:

> Dah language weh yuh proud o',
> Weh yuh honour and respeck,
> Po' Mass Charlie! Yuh noh know sey
> Dat it spring from dialect!

> Dat dem start fe try tun language,
> From de fourteen century,
> Five hundred years gawn an dem got
> More dialect dan we!

> Yuh wi haffe kill de Lancashire
> De Yorkshire, de Cockney
> De broad Scotch and de Irish brogue
> Before yuh start kill me!

> Yuh wi haffe get de Oxford book
> O' English verse, an tear
> Out Chaucer, Burns, Lady Grizelle
> An plenty o' Shakespeare!

Wen yuh done kill 'wit' an 'humour'
Wen yuh kill 'Variety'
Yuh wi haffe fine a way fe kill
Originality!

An mine how yuh dah-read dem English
Book deh pon yuh shelf
For ef yuh drop a 'h' yuh mighta
Haffe kill yuhself.

Similarly, Ranny Williams, who often shared a stage with Louise Bennett to perform Anancy stories, rebelled against being ashamed of his culture. He was descended from Maroons and rejected English cultural dominance. As he said in an interview: "The people were aiming after being polished and sophisticated, and the things that were English. They would watch and see how proper people conducted themselves and this was the way to behave. You shouldn't behave like going back towards slavery or something like that. We were moving towards the English pattern of behaviour and some people would rather be saying, 'The boy stood on the burning deck', you know, than saying, 'Gooma and Bredda Taku did gwain a one sort a ting downtown'."

Louise Bennett's stage and television persona of Miss Lou became enormously popular with children in Jamaica and, in *Jamaican Folk Tales and Oral Histories*, Laura Tanna describes her characteristic performance style: "An entire generation of Jamaican children have been raised watching Miss Lou entertain young ones on her popular *Ring Ding* television show. She encouraged members of the studio audience to sing, dance, and recite poetry in much the same way she must have done as a child, and always rewarded them with a loud 'Clap dem' as she led the audience applause. Often on the *Ring Ding* show, and periodically on short clips used as fillers, television viewers saw Miss Lou performing Anansi stories in her own particular style, eyes open wide in wonderment, hands held high as she gesticulates, her patois flying so fast from her tongue that one can scarcely keep up with the story until hearing the proverb she usually includes before her cheerful laugh punctuates the conclusion."

Michael Smith

Michael (Mikey) Smith was born in Kingston, Jamaica, on 14 September 1954. His father was a mason and his mother a factory worker. Although he went to several schools, Mikey claimed that most of his education was acquired on the street. He describes his school experience in 'Black and White':

> went to an all black school
> with an all black name
> all black principal
> black teacher
>
> graduated
> with an all black concept
>
> with our blackety blackety frustration
> we did an all black march
> with high black hopes
> and an all black song
>
> got a few solutions
> not all black
>
> went to a show
> and saw our struggles
> in black and white
>
> Lawwwwwd have mercy

He began writing as a child and filled a whole exercise book. But when he showed it to his father he was told that he could not make a living that way and his father burnt it all. His first performance was of a poem in which he attacked Ian Smith for his white minority rule in what was then Rhodesia. His ideas were influenced by Walter Rodney, the Guyanese radical, by Marcus Garvey and Langston Hughes.

Like Louise Bennett, he performed his poetry throughout the island at venues large and small, including youth clubs and community centres. He performed to great acclaim in Barbados, Britain, France,

Michael Smith

Holland and Italy, and through television and records his performances have become familiar to even more people. One of his most famous poems is 'Me Cyaan Believe It' which begins:

> Me seh me cyaan believe it
> me seh me cyaan believe it
>
> Room dem a rent
> me apply widin
> but as me go een
> cockroach rat an scorpion
> also come een
>
> Waan good
> nose haffi run
> but me naw go siddung pon high wall
> like Humpty Dumpty
> me a face me reality
>
> One little bwoy come blow im horn
> an me look pon im wid scorn
> an me realize how me five bwoy-picni
> was a victim of de trick
> dem call partisan politricks
>
> an me ban me belly
> an me bawl
> an me ban me belly
> an me bawl
> Lawd
> me cyaan believe it
> me seh me cyaan believe it

In an interview with Mervyn Morris, Mikey described how he got the idea for this poem:

> A man seh, "Boy, me can't believe it, that the thing gone up, you know." Me seh, "Rahtid, a it that, you

know! We can't believe it. And when you can't believe
it and you look and you see the things that you can't
believe." And then me go home now and me seh, "Yeh.
Poem now. I waan get a poem. 'Cyaan believe it'.
That's the poem I want." And then it slowly evolve. It
might work out. You might jot it down - line, piece a
line - and you go weh and you leave it, and then you
come back an you build on it. Or it might come 'roops',
right out. The whole intensity just come right out and
you just really - it release. Or sometimes a rhythm come
to me first. You know, is a rhythm, and me seh, "Dah
rhythm-ya feel nice, you know, feel nice." And then me
try remember the rhythm... and then I build under that,
build under that. Build under that and catch breaks and
the bridges. Just like how a musician a work out.

As Mervyn Morris says: "Listening to Mikey perform (with or without a
backing of music), one can hardly fail to notice his firm sense of structure
and of rhythmic patterning. The rhetoric of preachers and politicians, the
cries of pedlars; allusions to proverbs, nursery rhymes, children's games,
the Bible, Rasta talk, poems, reggae, and to flashpoints in Jamaican and
international news - they are pulled together or set against each other in
what are usually well articulated rhythmic structures."

From 1975, Michael Smith studied, at first part-time, at the Jamaica
School of Drama. In 1980, he graduated with a Diploma in Theatre
Arts. One of his tutors, Honor Ford Smith, explains how seriously he
took the preparations for his performances: "He would work hours
and hours, sometimes the whole day, with his tape recorder which
would have the backing tracks for the music, trying out different
variations of rhythm. He was very very conscious of the variety that
he could get in his voice. And you hear it in the voice, and you hear his
consciousness of pace, when you listen to his recording, and when
you hear him perform you would hear that he had worked for hours on
the pacing of his poetry, you know. So it wasn't just something that he
improvised when he got on stage."

On 17 August 1983, during the Jamaican election campaign, Michael
Smith was killed by four men at Stony Hill. When they stopped him in the
street, he told his attackers: "I-man free to walk anywhere in this land."

BLACK PERFORMANCE POETRY IN ENGLAND

London's burning

the sun comes out
in smiles
on black folk faces

Jean 'Binta' Breeze, *In the Heat of the Moment*, 1992

Chapeltown is where me come from
Where me use to sport me afro hair
An put on me flares
Where Blacker's sound
Had the sharpest lyrics around
And reggae music would a fill up the Chapeltown air.

Asher Hoyles, *Chapeltown*, 1997

Black hands, work all your life hands
unsteady now, savour memories
in a mango whilst time grows young again
on a park bench in Greenwich in June.

Joan Anim-Addo, *Summer Mango*, 1998

By the time Mikey Smith visited England in 1982, Black performance poetry was already established in the country. In particular, Linton Kwesi Johnson was writing and performing in the 1970s what became known as 'dub' or reggae poetry. Dub refers to the musical talkover of the DJs or toasters, and in Jamaica, poets such as Oku Onuora and Mutabaruka were performing in a similar style.

In *From Our Yard: Jamaican Poetry Since Independence* (1987), Pamela Mordecai writes that her anthology reflects two important trends in Jamaican poetry. One is the increased contribution of women;

"the other significant trend is that of oral or performance poetry, established by Louise Bennett, and developed, in one direction, by the new experimental form of 'dub'. Here that tradition is represented on the one hand in the work of Louise Bennett, James Berry and Valerie Bloom, and occasional poems of several other poets; on the other by the work of Linton Kwesi Johnson, Mutabaruka, Oku Onuora and Michael Smith."

In Trinidad, the 'dub' style is called 'rapso', related to the island's calypso tradition, which can be traced back to Yoruba songs. As the poet Brother Resistance explains: "Dub poetry and rapso, I see it as one family. The roots is the African oral tradition of ancient times, the griot. Rapso is a modern manifestation of this tradition just as dub poetry is. The slight difference, if you may call it that, is in terms of the musical influence. The riddum pattern of the rapso is more steeped in the Calypso/Soca, the riddum pattern of dub poetry is in reggae. But then again if you look at the musical connection you have one foundation which is drums. So it's the same thing with different accents of the same vibration."

Linton Kwesi Johnson came to England from Jamaica at the age of eleven and when he was about seventeen he joined the Black Panthers, the militant Black Power group which originated in the United States. After reading *The Souls of Black Folk* by W. E. B. Du Bois, he decided to write "to express and say something about what was going on in England with young people and how black people were being treated". He argued that what the reggae DJs were doing "was really poetry, and that it had a lot in common with traditional African poetry in so far as it was spontaneous, improvisatory and had a musical base".

He also explains the tension in his poems between different kinds of English: "The kind of thing that I write and the way I say it is as a result of the tension between Jamaican Creole and Jamaican English and between those and English English. And all that, really, is the consequence of having been brought up in a colonial society and then coming over here to live and go to school in England, soon afterwards. The tension builds up. You can see it in the writing. You can hear it. And something else: my poems may look sort of flat on the page. Well, that is because they're actually oral poems, as such. They were definitely written to be read aloud, in the community."

One of his earliest poems was 'Five Nights of Bleeding' which begins:

madness... madness...
madness tight on the heads of the rebels;
the bitterness erupts like a hot-blast.
broke glass;
rituals of blood on the burning,
served by a cruel in-fighting;
five nights of horror and of bleeding.
broke glass;
cold blades as sharp as the eyes of hate
and the stabbings.
it's war amongst the rebels:
madness... madness... war.

The sound systems of the 1970s were a source of inspiration for many Black people who later developed as poets, such as Benjamin Zephaniah, Levi Tafari and Asher. The sound system was not just a form of technology, but a whole cultural experience. It involved the technical ability to construct electrical circuits, carpentry skills to build speakers, artistry to paint and decorate them with signs and emblems, knowledge of the latest music (particularly from Jamaica), building up extensive record collections which would command respect, making innovations such as dub and echo systems, political and historical awareness (especially about Africa), improvisation and being able to chat conscious lyrics. The whole activity demonstrated that young Black people could plan, innovate and be self-reliant – all qualities that they were regularly being told by teachers that they did not possess.

By 1980, Benjamin Zephaniah had published his first book of poems, and the 1980s also saw mounting protests by the Black community against racism, discrimination and unemployment. In January 1981, thirteen young Black people were burnt to death in a house in New Cross, south London. The incident was commemorated by Linton Kwesi Johnson in his poem 'New Craas Massahkah'. On 2 March, 20,000 Black people marched the ten miles from New Cross to central London demanding justice for Black people. A few months later, towns up and down the country exploded in rebellion, the most powerful uprisings being by young Black people in the old slave ports of London, Bristol and Liverpool.

This is the context of the last twenty years, which, after the murder

Benjamin Zephaniah

of Stephen Lawrence in 1993, finally led the Macpherson Report to admit the existence of institutional racism throughout the country. The last twenty years have also seen a steady growth in the number and range of Black poets, who have written, among other things, about their situation as Black people in England.

They are also very conscious of their African heritage. Like Sojourner Truth, some Black poets have changed their names completely and others have added an African name to their existing names: for example Kamau (quiet warrior), Binta (beautiful daughter), Adisa (one who makes his meaning clear).

The subjects of their poems may not always be political, but the fact that they are writing at all is a political statement, as the Jamaican poet Edward Baugh makes clear:

> It was then he learned
> too late
> there's no such thing as '*only* literature'.
> Every line commits you.
> Those you thought dead will rise,
> accusing. And if you plead
> you never meant them,
> then feel responsibility
> break on you in a sudden sweat
> as the beast bears down.

Nevertheless, it is important to realise that the topics of performance poetry are as varied as any other poetry, especially as performance poetry has sometimes been criticised for only dealing with strident protest and ignoring other areas such as relationships, family, love, fantasy, humour. All these topics, however, can be found in the poetry in this book. It is also the case that many poets who do performance poetry also write poems in other styles which are not necessarily meant to be performed.

This book includes a selection of poets who are all actively committed to performing their poetry today. Each poet is profiled, and some of their favourite poems are included, both in text and audio.

This introduction has tried to explain some of the historical background to the poetry and hopefully this book will encourage an interest in reading and writing poetry, as well as performing and listening to it.

BENJAMIN ZEPHANIAH

Benjamin Zephaniah was born in 1958 in Coleshill, Warwickshire, and grew up in Handsworth, Birmingham. At school he and his twin sister were the only Black pupils and he would often be challenged to a fight. When he was nine, he and his mother, who worked as a nurse, left the rest of the family to live on their own.

He went to a series of schools, but hated them all. He was made captain of athletics, football, basketball, but he could not read or write, later discovering that he was also dyslexic. It was assumed by the teacher that he would be good at cricket:

>Teacher tell me
>I am good at cricket,
>I tell teacher
>I am not,
>Teacher tell me
>We luv cricket,
>I tell teacher
>Not me,
>I want Trigonometry
>Fe help me people,
>Teacher tell me
>I am a born Cricketer,
>But I never...... (well only once),
>I don't play cricket.

At school he was a rebel, always challenging the teachers. He was told by one teacher that Angela Davis was a terrorist. Thinking to himself, "this is the woman who is fighting for the freedom of black people in America who are being lynched", he promptly walked out of the class. Next day, he came back with 'Angela Davis' written on his jeans!

It was the time of the Biafran War in Nigeria and Benjamin remembers objecting to the racist jokes about starving Biafrans. He was very politically aware, always asking questions, disagreeing with his parents' view that church should be divorced from politics.

When a teacher told him that Columbus discovered America, he replied with a letter entitled 'Civil Lies':

> Dear Teacher,
>
> When I was born in Ethiopia
> Life began,
> As I sailed down the Nile civilization began,
> When I stopped to think universities were built,
> When I set sail
> Asians and true Americans sailed with me.
>
> When we traded nations were built,
> We did not have animals,
> Animals lived with us,
> We had so much time
> Thirteen months made our year,
> We created social services
> And cities that still stand.
>
> So teacher do not say
> Columbus discovered me
> Check the great things I was doing
> Before I suffered slavery.
>
> Yours truly,
>
> Mr Africa

He was finally expelled from school at the age of thirteen and never went back. There followed a series of petty crimes, approved school and prison, until, at the age of 21, he realised he needed to do more with his life. He enrolled in an Adult Education Class and eventually learnt to read and write.

Benjamin had been performing since the age of eleven - in church, where he was admired for his biblical knowledge and his ability to rap all the books of the bible. As he was illiterate, he would compose poems in his head. One of his first was 'Who's Who', about being a poet:

> I used to think nurses
> Were women
> I used to think police
> Were men
> I used to think poets
> Were boring
> Until I became one of them.

He describes one day finding a 'brother' in school who also liked poetry: "It was like if I was gay, finding someone else who's gay: 'You like poems too? Show me yours and I'll show you mine!' I'd drop one to him and then he'd drop one to me." He would also use poetry to approach the opposite sex: "If I wanted to chat up a girl in the playground – it's some rhymes I'm dropping on her."

Although he hated poetry at school, Benjamin liked listening to poets from Jamaica, like Louise Bennett. He also realised that there was another source of poetry close at hand: "On the sound systems most chatters were essentially poets - street poets. You had people doing the rhymes and toasting. But none of them called themselves poets because of the associations. It was later on we reclaimed the word."

His first poems were all very angry and his first political performances were on the streets of Handsworth, during anti-racist demonstrations when the National Front was marching. He says: "What unites all black people is the struggle. But lots of people have been a little bit tricked into thinking that the struggle is over because they've got a colour television and a nice job."

Since then, Benjamin has performed throughout the world and particularly likes visiting places like India, Zimbabwe and South Africa where there is still a strong oral tradition: "I do feel very much at home in India. In Britain, people will ask me why you are so political. Over there they will question you if you're not political: 'Look what's happening around you and you're writing about daffodils!'"

One of the main themes of his poetry is the police/Babylon and he explains this by referring to his own experience: "I remember being in a police station one night, being kicked by them, bleeding from the mouth. When I pissed, it was blood. I thought I was going to die. They kept me in there for days and it was illegal. Then they took me to court about four or five days later and said they arrested me the night before. I just remember being in there and being so alone and thinking they're getting away with it. The only way I could get revenge on them was to write my poems. I'll never forgive them for it."

Another interest is animals, and they appear a lot in his children's poetry. He has always loved animals and is a passionate vegan. One of his poems even tries to save the turkey from becoming Xmas dinner:

> Be nice to yu turkeys dis christmas
> Cos turkeys jus wanna hav fun
> Turkeys are cool, turkeys are wicked
> An every turkey has a Mum.
> Be nice to yu turkeys dis christmas,
> Don't eat it, keep it alive,
> It could be yu mate and not on yu plate
> Say, Yo! Turkey I'm on your side.

Of his performances, he says: "I've always known that I didn't just want to *read* poems, I wanted to *perform* poems. I don't use props – it's just me being physical. I do whatever it takes to bring the poem alive." When performing 'Dis Policeman Keeps on Kicking Me to Death', for example, he rolls around the floor, feet kicking, face distorted, dreadlocks flying.

> Like a bat from hell he comes at night
> To work his evil plan
> Although he goes to church on Sunday

> He's a sinner man,
> Like a thief in de dark he take me
> To de place where he just left
> And when him get me in der
> He is kicking me to death.
> Dis policeman, dis policeman
> Dis policeman keeps on kicking me to death.

He does not object to literary poetry: "I don't like to say one is better than the other. When literary people do that, they're making a big mistake. I always think of us as different branches of the same tree. If you want to get down to the roots of it - the oral tradition is older than the written tradition. We were talking before we were writing it down. I remember performing in Trafalgar Square and doing poems like 'Free South Africa' and 'Dis Policeman Keeps on Kicking Me to Death'. They were never published then and I had the audience chanting them with me. My poems were published in their hearts."

The same point is made in his poem 'Rapid Rapping':

> Long time agu before de book existed
> Poetry was oral an not playing mystic
> Poetry was something people understood
> Poetry was living in every neighbourhood
> Story telling was compelling listening, an entertaining
> Done without de ego trip an nu special training
> Found in many forms it was de oral tradition
> When governments said quiet, poets said no submission.

As regards publishing his poems he says: "I used to think it wasn't important to me, but then I realised that even in this age of video and visual aids, people want a book. People like to take a book into bed or to the toilet and kids want to read the stuff at school, especially as we're pioneering for black people here. In 200 years time they'll be looking back at the history of Black Britain and thinking these are the first black poets to be published in Britain."

At first, he did not want his poems to be taught in school – "they're for the street". But then he changed his mind: "I'll never forget one day a kid came up to me and said: 'Man, we need your poems in

school, cos of the bull-shit we're getting. I want some of you in school.'
Yeah, the guy's right, actually." He adds a warning, however: "We
need more teachers who are passionate about poetry, not just teachers
who do poetry as an add-on to English."

Benjamin Zephaniah lives in London's East End. Some of his
favourite poets are Shelley, Linton Kwesi Johnson and Maya Angelou;
some of the people who have influenced him most are Marcus Garvey,
Angela Davis and Malcolm X. His advice to budding poets is "be
honest and true to yourself":

> Jus one more ting before I go dat's yu can do it too
> Yu don't need fe read and write, be honest, loud and true.

DIS POETRY

Dis poetry is like a riddim dat drops
De tongue fires a riddim dat shoots like shots
Dis poetry is designed fe rantin
Dance hall style, Big mouth chanting,
Dis poetry nar put yu to sleep
Preaching follow me
Like yu is blind sheep,
Dis poetry is not Party Political
Not designed fe dose who are critical.

Dis poetry is wid me when I gu to me bed
It gets into me Dreadlocks
It lingers around me head
Dis poetry goes wid me as I pedal me bike
I've tried Shakespeare, Respect due dere
But dis is de stuff I like.

Dis poetry is not afraid of going ina book
Still dis poetry need ears fe hear an eyes fe hav a look
Dis poetry is Verbal Riddim, no big words involved
An if I hav a problem de riddim gets it solved,
I've tried to be more Romantic, it does nu good for me
So I tek a Reggae Riddim an build me poetry,
I could try be more personal
But you've heard it all before,
Pages of written words not needed
Brain has many words in store,
Yu could call dis poetry Dub Ranting
De tongue plays a beat
De body starts skanking,
Dis poetry is quick an childish
Dis poetry is fe de wise an foolish,
Anybody can do it fe free,
Dis poetry is fe yu an me,
Don't stretch yu imagination
Dis poetry is fe de good of de Nation,

Chant,
In de morning
I chant
In de night
I chant
In de darkness
An under de spotlight,
I pass thru University
I pass thru Sociology
An den I got a Dread degree
In dreadfull Ghettology.

Dis poetry stays wid me when I run or walk
An when I am talking to meself in poetry I talk,
Dis poetry is wid me,
Below me an above,
Dis poetry's from inside me
It goes to yu
WID LUV.

NO PROBLEM

I am not de problem
But I bare de brunt
Of silly playground taunts
An racist stunts,
I am not de problem
I am a born academic
But dey got me on de run
Now I am branded athletic,
I am not de problem
If yu give I a chance
I can teach yu of Timbuktu
I can do more dan dance,
I am not de problem
I greet yu wid a smile
Yu put me in a pigeon hole

But I am versatile.

These conditions may affect me
As I get older,
An I am positively sure
I have no chips on me shoulder,
Black is not de problem
Mother country get it right,
An juss fe de record,
Sum of me best friends are white.

I HAVE A SCHEME

I am here today my friends to tell you there is hope
As high as that mountain may seem
I must tell you
I have a dream
And my friends
There is a tunnel at the end of the light.
And beyond that tunnel I see a future
I see a time
When angry white men
Will sit down with angry black women
And talk about the weather,
Black employers will display notice-boards proclaiming,
'Me nu care wea yu come from yu know
So long as yu can do a good day's work, dat cool wid me.'

I see a time
When words like affirmative action
Will have sexual connotations
And black people all over this blessed country of ours
Will play golf,
Yes my friends that time is coming
And in that time
Afro-Caribbean and Asian youth
Will spend big money on English takeaways

And all police officers will be armed
With a dumplin,
I see a time
A time when the President of the United States of
          America will stand up and say,
'I inhaled
And it did kinda nice
So rewind and cum again.'
Immigration officers will just check that you are all
          right
And all black people will speak Welsh.

I may not get there my friends
But I have seen that time
I see thousands of muscular black men on
          Hampstead Heath walking their poodles
And hundreds of black female Formula 1 drivers
Racing around Birmingham in pursuit of a truly
          British way of life.
I have a dream
That one day from all the churches of this land we
          will hear the sound of that great old
          English spiritual,
Here we go, Here we go, Here we go.
One day all great songs will be made that way.

I am here today my friends to tell you
That the time is coming
When all people, regardless of colour or class, will
          have at least one Barry Manilow record
And vending-machines throughout the continent of
          Europe
Will flow with sour sap and sugarcane juice,
For it is written in the great book of multiculturalism
That the curry will blend with the shepherd's pie
          and the Afro hairstyle will return.

Le me hear you say

Multiculture
Amen
Let me hear you say
Roti, Roti
A women.

The time is coming
I may not get there with you
But I have seen that time,
And as an Equal Opportunities poet
It pleases me
To give you this opportunity
To share my vision of hope
And I just hope you can cope
With a future as black as this.

VALERIE BLOOM

Valerie Bloom was born Valerie Wright, in 1956, in a village called Frankfield in Clarendon, Jamaica. She had a wonderful childhood spent in a very big extended family: "There were nine of us, including cousins, and when you wanted to play games, you always had someone to play with and to share chores."

Her favourite subject at school was English and the poetry she read was mainly from England, for example Keats and Wordsworth: "We just had to memorise them and recite them and that was poetry. I loved poetry, but many people didn't because it was just like a chore. What I liked about it was the rhythm and the interesting use of words, so I used to learn poems without being told. I was fascinated with poetry from the beginning. I used to try and write in the style of Keats and Wordsworth, but my brothers and sisters fell about laughing when they heard my attempts!"

Valerie now spends most of her time visiting schools in Britain and Ireland, performing her poetry, and she has noticed a change in students' attitude to poetry: "In the past, children used to see poetry as a bind. It was something they didn't understand and they weren't taught it properly. The teachers themselves were not taught how to teach poetry and, not being poets themselves, it was something new to them. They passed on their own reserves about poetry without really knowing it.

"Nowadays, all that is changing because there's so much more emphasis on enjoyment and so much more knowledge of poetry appreciation. You get poets going into schools now. Before, children didn't meet the poets and weren't able to ask them questions about their poems. There's much more interaction between the makers of poetry and the users of poetry these days. Also, there's a lot more travelling now and sharing of cultures. You get more performance poetry now, which we didn't have before. That gives the children scope for taking part in the poetry, but also for making poetry - they get so much pleasure from making poems with the poets. When I first started going into schools and said we're going to write some poetry together, you'd hear a big groan go up! Nowadays, when I say we're going to write some poetry, the children actually go 'Yesss!'"

Valerie's first poem was published when she was twelve, in a children's newspaper, but she doesn't remember writing it: "So, I always say to people that the first poem I wrote was when I was in my teens. That won a medal in the National Festival in Jamaica and the next year there were school children all over the island reciting the poem and getting gold medals at the Festival for it. So that's what really started me writing. Although I love poetry, I always wanted to write prose. From the time I could write, I was writing stories and I was always top of the class because of the stories. A lot of my poems now are narrative poems."

Before training as a teacher, Valerie worked as a librarian for a year, then, after college, she went back to teach in Frankfield where, in addition to teaching English, Speech, Drama and Home Economics, she started a Speech and Drama Club. In 1979, she came to England and met up with a group of Jamaicans who had left Jamaica in the 1950s and 1960s: "They wanted to start a folk-singing group, but they couldn't remember the words of the folk songs, so, hearing that I had just come over from Jamaica, they asked if I could come and help them. I started teaching them folk songs and choreographing, and pretty soon they were being asked all over the country to come and sing. I would go with them and just as a bit of variation I would do a poem as part of the show. So then people kept asking me to come and do some poems and when I went they said, 'Where's the book?'

"So I went to Bogle-L'Ouverture publishers, and said, 'I've got these poems. Would you be interested in publishing them?' They said yes and that was my first book, *Touch Mi! Tell Mi!*, published in 1983." One of the poems in this collection is 'Wha fe Call i'' describing the confusion about what to call meals at different times of the day. For instance, is the meal at midday, dinner or lunch?

Miss Ivy, tell mi supmn,
An mi wan' yuh ansa good.
When yuh eat round 12 o'clock,
Wassit yuh call yuh food?

For fram mi come yah mi confuse,
An mi noh know which is right,
Weddah dinnah a de food yuh eat midday,
Or de one yuh eat a night.

As performance is part of Jamaican culture, Valerie came to it very early: "We have story-telling sessions and everybody would get up and tell a story and that would be a performance. Poetry was never read, it was always performed. We used to have tea parties at school where the school would put on a session to raise funds. There would be people performing and some food: curry goat and rice an' peas. At one of these tea parties they asked me to do a poem and I did a Louise Bennett poem. All Jamaican children would learn Louise Bennett poems. It was the one kind of poetry they would just learn without being told, because it was in their own language. That was the first performance I remember and it was reported in the paper next day." Since then, she has also performed in other Caribbean islands such as St Lucia and Dominica.

Although her poems come from the oral tradition, Valerie likes to see them published as this makes them available to many more people. Some of them have been included in the GCSE syllabus, which has given her the opportunity to travel round the country, often to places such as Cornwall or Ireland where few Black people live. She can also, then, explain that patois is a proper language and not just broken English, as so many people still believe. This point is illustrated in her poem 'Language Barrier'.

Louise Bennett has been the strongest influence on Valerie's poetry, especially in the early days. Other favourite poets are Charles Causley from Cornwall, who writes "beautiful children's poetry", Maya Angelou, Jean 'Binta' Breeze, Merle Collins from Grenada, and the American, Langston Hughes.

One of her favourite poems is 'The Listeners' by Walter de la Mare, which begins:

'Is there anybody there?' said the Traveller,
　　Knocking on the moonlit door;
And his horse in the silence champed the grasses
　　Of the forest's ferny floor.

Another is Robert Frost's 'Stopping By Woods On A Snowy Evening',
which ends:

The woods are lovely, dark and deep.
But I have promises to keep,
And miles to go before I sleep,
And miles to go before I sleep.

She has also written a poem inspired by Thomas Hood's poem 'No'. It
is called 'De' and describes an English winter. It begins:

De snow, de sleet, de lack o' heat,
De wishy-washy sunlight,
De lip turn blue, de cold, 'ACHOO!'
De runny nose, de frostbite,

De creakin' knee, de misery,
De joint dem all rheumatic,
De icy bed (de blanket dead),
De burs' pipe in de attic.

Valerie usually writes various drafts of a poem in a notebook: "I write
on trains or in hotel rooms. Sometimes I have a poem in my head
going round for a long time before I write it down. Sometimes I write
part of a poem and it won't go any further. It just stops and you know
you have to put it away and come back to it some other time.

　"One of my favourite poems for children is 'Sandwich'. I started
that poem in about 1993, but I got stuck and it wouldn't budge, so I
just put it down. Then, last year, I was on a train and I had it with me
and the poem just flowed out. It's different from how I started it, but
so much better. You can't force the poem and your sub-conscious is
working away all the time without you realising it."

　As for inspiration, Valerie quotes the saying that success depends ten percent on inspiration and ninety percent on perspiration! She often feels a greater power is guiding her: "I'm usually working on a lot of things at once, so if I get bogged down on one I just work on something else. What you need to do is relax and read a lot, go out and see other people, see a show, listen to other poets."

An important theme in her poetry is food, which she sees as an important part of her culture, a social occasion. In the following poem 'Granny Is', she recalls the food associated with her grandmother: 'run-dung', a sauce made from coconut cream and seasoning, usually cooked with meat or fish; coconut drops, diced coconut cooked in spiced caramel; and grater cake, a sweet made from grated coconut, spice and sugar:

> Granny is
> fried dumplin' an' run-dung,
> coconut drops an' grater cake,
> fresh ground coffee smell in the mornin'
> when we wake.

Another theme is duppies, as in 'Duppy Jamboree' where a child is frightened by the Jonkunnu carnival celebrations, thinking there are ghosts outside:

> What that noise me hearing
> Coming from out o' doah?
> Mi get out o' bed, pull back de curtain
> An' peep out tru de window.
>
> Me rub me yeye an' look again,
> Can't believe wha me just see,
> Twenty-seven duppy dere
> Staring back at me!
>
> One o' dem stand up dere
> With him head under him arm
> One o' dem is a big ole bull
> Like de one pon Granpa farm.

In 'Duppy Story Time', which illustrates the Jamaican oral tradition, the children are thrilled and frightened at the same time by granny's story. The poem begins:

> The breeze a-blow cool, the night it dark,
> But none o' we no worry,
> For we siddung roun' the fire,
> An Granny a-tell we duppy story.

It ends with granny wanting to tell another story:

> But none o' we no hear Granny
> We jump eena we bed,
> Say we prayers, turn up the lamp
> An pull the sheet over we head.
>
> We teeth a-rattle, we knee dem a-tremble
> We dying now with fright,
> We will never lissen to another duppy story
> (Until tomorrow night).

Valerie believes there's no time like the present: "Many people say they want to write poetry and it's always in the future, so you have to say, 'Write it now. Get it done!' Also, a lot of people write poetry and they don't read poetry. You cannot make a cabinet without being taught how to do it, reading the manual or going to school. Poetry is your job and you need to learn it in the same way. So read as much as you can, because you learn from other people; and go and see performances.

"There are many exercises to get your sub-conscious working. One is to write for five minutes on a particular title without thinking too much and don't let the pen off the paper till the five minutes are up. Then you just put it away and the next day you look at it and you'll be amazed to see what comes out.

"There are many training courses now which I didn't have. Grab hold of them because it's such an opportunity. Remember not everything you write is going to be good. Most of what you write is going to be no good! But you musn't get disheartened, because out of that the gems will come. It's like digging for pearls. You don't get pearls from off the surface. You have to dig deep for the best ones."

SANDWICH

We goin' on a school trip today,
De whole class goin' to Whitney Bay,
Ah teckin' me ball an' bat with me
To play beach cricket, an' let me see,
Ah mustn't forget me new frisbee,
An teacher say to bring a sandwich.

She say to bring a waterproof mac,
An' a change o' clothes in a knapsack,
For it bound to rain, she guarantee,
An' half o' we gwine end up in the sea,
An' we mustn't forget, any o' we,
Teacher say, to bring a sandwich.

She say we can bring a can o' drink,
Ah will bring some fizzy orange, ah think,
Some gobstoppers ah can share with Lee,
(An' everybody else, probably)
An apple or orange, an', ah definitely
Won't forget to bring a sandwich.

Ah ask me mother for some bread,
Some butter, lettuce, an' some ched-
dar cheese, don't need nothing more,
An' ah just headin' for the door
When ah bump into me Granny Lenore,
An' she teck away me sandwich.

She say, don't know what you mother thinkin' 'bout,
How she could let a growin' child go out
With one little sandwich alone to eat,
But don't you worry, chile, in this basket,
I have corn pone, chicken an' jerk meat,
You don't need to teck a sandwich.

Ah say to her, you don't understan',
Ah cannot teck all of dem things, Gran,
De whole o' de class will laugh at me,
She say, I do you favourite fricassee,
Ah tell her, Gran, teacher specifickly
Say dat we must bring a sandwich.

But she not listening to a thing
Me say. She waltz pass me an' den she bring
Out a bowl o' rice an' peas,
A whole hardo bread, if you please,
Ah was down on the floor, pon me hands an' knees
Beggin', give me back me sandwich.

Den Gran teck out a thermos flask,
Ah shut me yeye, ah fraid to ask,
But ah wonder what next she woulda produce,
She say, look, some nice soursop juice,
So gimme dat fizzy nonsense, dat's no use,
And she teck it, jus like me sandwich.

Gran, yuh have enough to feed de whole class dere,
She say, dat is right, yuh must learn to share,
Ah put something in for you teacher too,
And she pull out a bowl o' callaloo,
Ah ax meself, what ah going to do?
Ah only want to teck a sandwich.

No matter how me beg an' plead,
She was like a mad bull on stampede,
So wid chicken, rice an' hardo bread,
Me heart an' foot dem heavy like lead,
Ah wave goodbye to me street cred,
An lef' without me sandwich.

All day ah try to pretend
Ah didn' know dat basket, but in the end
Lunch time come an' we all gather roun',

Spread some blanket on the groun'
An' everybody settle down,
To open up dem sandwich.

Teacher say, 'What have you got there?'
Ah pretend ah didn' hear,
But dat basket wouldn' go away,
So ah open it an' start to pray
Dat they wouldn' laugh too loud when ah display
What ah bring instead o' sandwich.

Well everybody yeye dem near pop out,
My friend Lee start to lick him mout',
So ah ask dem if dey all want some,
Dey look pon me like ah really dumb,
In no time we finish every crumb,
An' dem all feget dem sandwich.

When teacher say, 'Thank your grandmother for us',
Ah feel so proud, ah nearly bus',
She say, 'That was a really super meal',
Everybody say, 'Yeah, that was well cool, Neil',
An' yuh don' know how glad ah feel
Dat ah didn' bring - a sandwich.

YUH HEAR BOUT

Yuh hear bout di people dem arres
Fi bun dung di Asian people dem house?
Yuh hear bout de policeman dem lock up
Fi beat up di black bwoy widout a cause?
Yuh hear bout di M.P. dem sack because im
     refuse fi help
im black constituents in a dem fight
     'gainst deportation?
Yuh noh hear bout dem?
Me neida.

LANGUAGE BARRIER

Jamaica language sweet yuh know bwoy,
An yuh know mi nebba notice i',
Till tarra day one foreign frien'
Come spen some time wid mi.

An den im call mi attention to
Some tings im sey no clear,
Like de way wi always sey 'koo yah'
When we really mean 'look here'.

Den annodda ting whey puzzle im,
Is de way wi always repeat wi-se'f,
For de ongle time im repeat a wud
Is when smaddy half deaf.

Todda day im a walk outa road
An when im a pass one gate,
Im see one bwoy a one winda,
As one nodda outside a wait.

Im sey dem did look frien'ly
Soh im ben a go sey howdy,
But im haffe tap when de fus' bwoy sey
"A ready yuh ready aready"

Den like sey dat nebba enuff
Fe po' likkle foreign Hugh,
Him hear de nedda bwoy halla out,
"A come mi come fe come wait fe yuh"

An dat is not all dat puzzle im,
Why wi run wi words togedda?
When im expec' fe hear "the other",
Im hear dis one word, "todda".

Some o' de expression dem im hear,

Im no badda try fe meck dem out,
Like "boonoonoonos", "chamba-chamba",
An "kibba up yuh mout".

Im no know ef dem a cuss or praise im
When people call im "preckey",
An im cyan wuk out de connection
Between "only" and "dengey".

Mi tell Hugh nuffe teck awn soh'
Nuffe badda run wi dung,
Is not dat wi don like English
But wi lub wi modda tongue.

Eena France, Italy, Spain an Greece
Dem guilty o' de same crime,
Soh ef Hugh gwine keep on travel
Im betta larn fe mime.

But sayin dis an dat, yuh know,
Sometime wi cyan undastan one anodda,
Even doah wi all lib yah
An chat de same patwa.

For all now mi no' undastan
Whey Joey mean yessiday,
When as mi come een from wuk im wake up
Soh ax mi whey im dinna dey.

GLOSSARY

boonoonoonos	pretty, desirable, attractive
chamba-chamba	ragged, tatty
kibba up	literally 'cover up', close, shut
preckey	person of no account
dengey	single

JOHN LYONS

John Lyons was born in 1933 in Port of Spain, Trinidad. He lived right in the centre of the city and, when he was four years old, he was shown the way to his school so that he could walk there on his own. Years later, he returned and wrote:

> And where is the old nursery school
> on George Street in Port-of-Spain,
> shuttered and locked against rioters
> back in '38 when Charlie King
> was burnt alive in a Southern oil field?
> ('The Return')

His father made shoes:

> You cobbled morning, noon and night,
> work was a striding to your grave.
> All you bequeathed was the memory
> of your ways.
> ('A Poem for my Father')

He also supplied other shoemakers with leather. One of these men used to tease John on his way to school: "This guy had a very twisted sense of humour. He would see me in my shirt-tails and pull out his shoemaker's knife to cut them off. My father got angry and stopped him doing it, but he tried something else. I had to go past a saw-mill cutting tropical cedar, the sawdust of which, when mixed with the water of the gutter, ran a reddish colour. The mill was all barred up, you couldn't see what was happening, you just heard this noise and you saw this red stuff coming out. He said to me that they killed little boys in there. I didn't say anything to my father, but I had to go past there every single day. It was terrible. It's things like that which etch themselves into your psyche, which eventually produce a poem."

> He turned to ambush then,
> on my proud way
> to nursery school on the block,
> past the cedar saw-mill.
>
> It was he who changed
> that saw-mill to a monster
> with appetite for little boys.
> Mill gutters ran blood
> the colour of water stained with cedar.
> ('Riptix, the Itinerant Cobbler')

John's mother died when he was nine: "That was quite a traumatic experience. I was the eldest and I had one brother and two sisters. We went to Tobago to live with our grandmother, who was already looking after one child. That was a totally different life, coming from a city to a smaller island, very rustic, very beautiful. There was a lot of bush around and I had to learn how to avoid stepping on snakes. I became really hyped up in terms of my senses. I knew, when I went into the bush, if a snake had gone past. I could smell it. The experiences I had there were very rich for my writing and I'm still writing about them."

> Amidst bush and bramble
> I grew wild as rocksage, learned
> how to avoid stepping on snakes.
> ('Tobago Days')

Returning many years later by aeroplane, he describes the view as the plane landed:

> Tobago from this height was no larger
> than a green postage stamp.
>
> Our quick descent telescoped the green,
> magnified it to cultivated fields,
> trees spattered with blossoms, bright birds.
>
> In a field embroidered with furrows
> a scarlet ibis flaunted its landing skills.
> ('Landing on Crusoe's Island')

His grandmother was "a very strong Victorian lady, very tall and strapping. She said she feared nobody at all - only God, no man. She brought us up very strict and often after school, when other kids were playing out, I was in the garden hoeing and weeding and she was standing there making sure I did it properly."

> Weekdays after school were a burden
> of chores: With hoe and rake
> I bullied the soil between cassava beds,
> toted firewood on head pad,
> filled water barrels while I hastened
> the night with hard wishing.
> ('Tobago Days')

"I had a very hard, strict upbringing. She gave us respect for authority and also obedience, respect for adults and a very strong respect for education. That was so important. There was an hour set aside for everybody, after you had finished your chores, to sit at the table and read and work and do our sums."

> Then it is time to sit around table on rough-hewn
> benches,
> to eat slices of johnny-bakes daubed with salty,
> orange-coloured margarine, drink herb tea,
>
> and after, to do our sums or read silently
> under threat of Tom Stickley, the harness leather strap

rigid in Granma's lap.
('Tobago Twilight')

John's aunt, who was a teacher, gave him a card for the library, which was only two or three miles away. At the age of ten or eleven, he started to read novels, such as *Quentin Durward* and other novels by Walter Scott: "I became a book-worm. I didn't do my chores, but used to hide up a tree to read. I lived everything I read. For instance, when I read *Robin Hood*, I actually made my own bow and arrow and my own quiver. I made a hat and went out into the bush imagining I was Robin Hood. In school we had to learn a lot of poetry by heart, for example Rudyard Kipling, works chosen by our colonial masters. We also had to recite the poems. I liked looking at plants, anything to do with nature. I also liked drawing very much and got into trouble with my father for using my exercise books for drawing instead of for sums!"

In his twenties, John came to England and between 1959 and 1964 studied art at Goldsmiths College in London. He remembers reading some of the poems, which he had brought over with him, to his fellow students: "They laughed me to scorn. They said they were romantic and belonged to the past. That brought me up short. I stopped writing for a time, but carried on reading and making notes. I look back at my first poems with a great deal of embarrassment because I wasn't precise enough in my use of language."

Writing poetry is a lengthy business: "I walk around with my notebook, always scribbling in it. Then I go over and over the notes and draft it in long hand. There will be about seven drafts and then I put it on the computer and do a few more drafts. Then I leave it for a while and when I come back to it I may change it again. The excitement is not in the end product, the poem, but in the getting there, sorting it out. If I have the slightest doubt about it, I have to re-write it until I think I've done my best. Sometimes I can't pull my notes together. I try something and it doesn't work. Then in the middle of doing something quite different, like washing up, it comes and you have to go back to it."

He believes in the words of the American poet William Carlos Williams: "No idea but in things" ('A Sort of a Song'). By this, he understands that you must always stress the particular: "A strong philosophical idea needs to be tied to something ordinary, a metaphor, something to make it accessible, so that when people read it, it seems simple. You have to try and encapsulate that very grand, universal idea in something that is simple and recognised by everyone. Being a poet is a way of life. It's part of the way you perceive things, it's a change of consciousness. You look at things differently. Having the skill to play with words - you cannot create until you play."

John's first performance was with Valerie Bloom in Manchester and he remembers how his grandmother had always encouraged him to perform: "She always wanted me to sing or perform and when I didn't get a part in a play, she used to go into the school and demand I be given one!"

He has since performed his poems at festivals all over the country, including Scotland, Ireland and Wales, as well as on television. He sees the importance of performance poetry in the way you have eye contact with people, your movement and body language, the direct communication you have with the audience: "This comes from Caribbean culture, street theatre, nation language and the different rhythms like calypso."

At the same time, he likes to see his poems published: "We have the oral tradition, but our whole education was based on what was in books. I was very pleased when I got my work published, when I could see it there in a book – it's an object, it's a physical thing. I can give it to people. I can sell it. It's there on the shelf in a library or in a bookshop. But it doesn't mean that people who are not published are not poets."

His favourite poets are Derek Walcott, Kamau Brathwaite and R.S. Thomas whom he likes for his "honesty in putting down on paper his doubts and recognising the dark side of life, which gives you a shiver when you read him". He also likes Grace Nichols, Carol Ann Duffy, Jean 'Binta' Breeze, Valerie Bloom and the Welsh poet Gillian Clarke.

One of his favourite poems is 'The Schooner *Flight*' by Derek Walcott:

> In idle August, while the sea soft,
> and leaves of brown stick to the rim
> of this Caribbean, I blow out the light

by the dreamless face of Maria Concepcion
to ship as a seaman on the schooner *Flight*.

. . . .

You ever look up from some lonely beach
and see a far schooner? Well, when I write
this poem, each phrase go be soaked in salt;
I go draw and knot every line as tight
as ropes in this rigging; in simple speech
my common language go be the wind,
my pages the sails of the schooner *Flight*.

John Lyons is an artist as well as a poet, and he has exhibited his
paintings abroad in Holland and France. He has also been a lecturer in
art at the South Trafford College in Manchester. He now lives in Hebden
Bridge, West Yorkshire, where he runs creative writing workshops:
"You can't *teach* anybody to write or paint, but you can guide and
suggest how people can tap into their memories and experience, what
mechanisms they can use to do that. I have done that - visualisation
meditation, to get into a different part of you mind."

Some of the major themes of his poetry are the jumbie bird,
soucouyant and carnival, all of which represent the darker side of life.
The jumbie bird is an owl that utters an eerie shriek as it flies low,
hunting at night, so giving rise to a strong superstition that it is a
messenger of death:

Night is a bed of dreams.
I mould the darkness
into images I can touch:
Skin hairs become feathers,
eyes dilate, fill my face;

I am a jumbie bird
in connivance with the night
twisting dreams
into nightmares.
('Metamorphosis')

In Trinidad, soucouyant disguises as a wrinkled old woman during the day, but at night takes off her skin, hides it in a cool place and becomes a ball of fire. She seeks sleeping victims whose blood she sucks and then she must return to her skin before sunrise to avoid dying.

> The ball of fire
> broke into his night
>
> and on his neck the dry ice
> of a kiss
> sucking his blood away.
> ('The Soucouyant Visitation')

Carnival, too, hides a dark history:

> Behind the carnival
> jumbie owls screech.
> They see what no masquerader sees:
> the portent in Bad-behaviour sailors' dance,
> 'Las lap we go beat massa-massa,
> las lap we go beat massa-massa.'
>
> Behind the carnival
> the dragon menaces;
> but he is chained by steel
> tempered in the hell of sugar plantations
> and must learn to dance calypso.
> 'Hold the dragon,
> hold the dragon,'
> behind the carnival.
> ('Behind the Carnival')

His advice to new poets is: "Enjoy the process of writing and read as much as you write. Find poets you like."

THE MAN OF THE HOUSE

He had a maco tongue in he mouth
but this time he went too far.
I give-im ah piece ah meh mine.
'If she was here,' I said, 'she wouldn't
want yuh to call she, Tun-Tun'.

He got vex, said how
Caribbean women dohn need
alladat feminist nonsense,
How they strong strong
and in high position in the islands.

That night when he came home
he found a raw breast of chicken.
Pinned to it was a scribbled note:
'Yuh food. Gone to lime with my
sisters in the women's club.'

His cussin set the dogs
in the neighbourhood barking.

DEY IS KIATS AN KIATS

Kiats in Englan!
Dey spoil, *oui*:
dey laugh an play
hide-an-seek wid mice;
buh lehme tell yuh something,
in de Caribbean,
we different altogedder.

Frastart, we always hungry
- as real kiats should be.
Wen we huntin,
we fass like lightnin
ready fuh anyting dat move.

On de odderhan,
here in Englan kiat get fat
on tin food from supermarkit;
man, dey losin all selfrespeck:
dey dohn even begin to know
how to ketch mice;
an dey ha de brassface to believe
dey better dan we back home.

Yuh know wat I tink!
- I go tell yuh anyway –
because dey go to dem beauty salon
to get deself dollsup,
because dey geh deself sterelise,
dey tink dey modern an liberated,
eh heh, ah know wah ah talking bout
ah tellin yuh,

I hear dem wid meh own ears:
dey call we Caribbean kiats,
'primitive wild beasts',
well, dat mek meh laugh;
we so-called wild beasts
dohn en up in de vet all de time,
we live natural and healty,
free as a bird;
well, free anyway.

SOUCOUYANT ON BONFIRE NIGHT

Wen de bangers
An rockets
An pungent air
Keep sleep away,
Jus stare in de sky.
Yuh go barely see
A comet flyin low
Is Soucouyant
Camouflage
In bonfire glow.

Soucouyant
Soucouyant
Wey yuh dey
Ah know yuh hidin
In de fire
An yuh not burnin.

Soucouyant find comfort
In dis nite explodin
An wid no caution
Fling sheself in flight
Wid she vampire attire
A red an orange
Ball-a-fire.

Soucouyant
Soucouyant
Wey yuh dey
Ah know yuh hidin
In de fire
An yuh not burnin.

Watch out
Watch out
Soucouyant want to kiss yuh

Wid she hot, hot mout
Leave yuh wid dreams
Leave yuh on fire.

Soucouyant
Soucouyant
Wey yuh dey
Ah know yuh hidin
In de fire
An yuh not burnin.

ANCESTORS SAY GOODBYE

The boat's 'boooooooom'
In the bay bounced off hills,
Joined ancestral voices:
'Dey leavin, dey leavin,
dey leavin de bush,
dove siesta lullabys.'

'Dey leavin sweet potato
to rootin pigs.
yams to run wild,
gully-root and shado-beni.'

'Dey leavin ajoupas
huggin cool valleys,
shacks clingin to slopes
topside of seaside fishin town.'

'Dey leavin de city bazodee
Wid its chantin poitique,
Wid its rumble an dust.'

'Wey yuh goin,
wey yuh goin?'
ancestral voices whisper

like wind through
poui and poinciana.

'Wey yuh goin,
wey yuh rushin to?'
But dey dohn look at de lan;
Dey leavin wid ruction
In dey head.

Lan weepin,
Crapaud in de house
In dark under de bed.
Cat gone,
Dog stray.

'But wey yuh goin,
wey yuh goin
leavin happy rain,
days wash clean,
sun-polished days?

'Wey yuh goin,
wey yuh goin
after all dem years
groin up wid breadfruit
an roast salfish? I tellin yuh,
yuh go miss yuh limin
an yuh bacchanal.'

The wind rush across the Atlantic
Like it malkadie, push water
Into shifting hills,
Into moving gullies.
Wind wild, wild
Wid more power dan de obeahman.

De Empire Windrush
Like it tootoolbay

Lurchin like a jack mule on de ocean,
Sailin one side
Of de slave trade triangle
Wind loud like vexation;
But dis time no dead cargo
To feed de greedy sharks.

Dis time dey on dey feet
dancin on deck,
Singin sex rhythms,
Bush rum visions in dey heads.
'No more catchin we nennen.' Dey say.
Opportunity,
Opportunity
In de modder country.

GLOSSARY

gully-root	tall weed with tiny white flowers, used as folk-medicine
shado-beni	fit-weed, wild herb used to cure fevers and fits
ajoupa	Amerindian-type hut with thatched roof
bazodee	confusion
poitique	vendor
poui	large shade tree with masses of pink or yellow flowers
poinciana	plant with flame-coloured flowers
crapaud	toad
limin	chilling out, loafing and chatting
bacchanal	rave, noisy merry-making
malkadie	epileptic fit
tootoolbay	dazed or bewitched
catchin we nennen	having great difficulty making ends meet

ASHER HOYLES

Asher Hoyles, whose mother comes from Nevis, was born in Leeds on 12 December 1966. She was brought up in Chapeltown and had a strict childhood. At a very early age, she had responsibilities around the house, such as cooking and cleaning, which were sometimes carried out reluctantly because she longed to be playing outside.

In primary school, she realised she had the ability to tell stories and liked writing them too. She remembers writing a poem and winning some sweets in a competition, but it was not really encouraged. Asher also liked listening to stories and particularly remembers a teacher, called Mr Nelson, reading *Catweazle*, doing all the characters in their different voices. She enjoyed going swimming and played the violin until it was stolen from the school. At secondary school, she liked drama and remembers being in *A Midsummer Night's Dream* and Brecht's *Caucasian Chalk Circle*, produced by her art teacher David Wood.

On the whole, however, she did not like school subjects and was lacking in self-confidence. She later wrote a poem about school called 'Ting a Ling' which challenged the view that your schooldays are the best days of your life:

> I remember dat lie
> wid forty children in de class
> routine task
> teacher a bawl
> how ungrateful we are

me hatred of maths
being bottom of the class
answering back
getting a slap.

On Saturdays, Asher went with her mother to the Seventh Day Adventist church where Sister Baker often used to ask her to recite poems and passages from the bible: "I had to learn them by heart. I knew people liked to hear me, so there must have been something about my voice that people approved of. I remember going up there and my mum sitting there looking proud. It was all about being the best that you can. I learnt standards. You had to do it well. It was the same with cooking. You had to make sure you did things to the best of your ability."

Another experience of performing came about when Asher was fourteen: "Chatting lyrics on the mic in Chapeltown was my earliest experience of poetry, though we never called it that. The fact of being a woman was important too, and getting respect from the male MCs."

She also received some informal education: "Educationally, we weren't brought up to understand anything about our history or background. Rastaman was coming forward with a new perspective on things that made me inquisitive. What was this place called Africa? What's this thing about roots? I was being told I belonged somewhere and that felt really good, even though I didn't know where to find Africa on a map! That was positive. I was growing up where people were saying, 'Go back to your own country!' Where? I was born here! It was all very confusing and all I used to say was 'It's not fair!'"

When I was a yout an living in Yorkshire
I never knew a thing about my African culture
The first time I came across the term retention
I really did believe it was a physical condition
It was only when I listened to the music of the rasta
And I heard in the lyrics we were going back to Africa.
('Retention Attention')

At the age of sixteen, Asher left Leeds for London, but it was not until some years later when she went to university that she started writing poetry: "I always had difficulty writing and at university I discovered

I was dyslexic. Poetry became important to me as a way of expressing things in the way that I wanted to. I wanted to stamp my own voice on things. I'd previously written songs for bands I had been in. Then I started to show my friend, Michael, some of my poems and he gave me a lot of encouragement."

The poetry was very therapeutic: "I always wanted to be committed to something and strangely being dyslexic led to an interest in writing poetry to express how I was feeling. I was very tense at that time and writing poetry got rid of a lot of frustrations. At last I was beginning to find my own voice and I was becoming more politically aware. I realised I had so much to say."

The first poem she wrote was called 'Hot Water in Your Place', about responsibilities in the home:

> When I was a child
> My mother used to have a golden rule
> She used to say
> Always have hot water in your place
> Not just for cooking
> But for your emergencies.

Her first performance was at Bunjie's in Charing Cross Road: "It was the most nerve-wracking experience, hands sweating, very shaky and nervous, scared out of my wits. My next venue was Chat's Palace in Hackney, with a mainly black audience. I was very frightened, but when people came up afterwards and asked me questions about my poetry, it was very encouraging. It makes you want to do more."

Since then, she has performed at many venues including the Hay-on-Wye festival, the Institute of Contemporary Arts, Survivors' Poetry, Stratford Circus and on the street at the Stoke Newington summer festival. She has been to schools and colleges, libraries and community centres, pubs and clubs, and led poetry workshops at Maidstone Men's Prison and Rayleigh Women's Prison. Her poems have also been displayed on London buses. In October 2001, she was proud to share a platform in Camden with John la Rose, of New Beacon, and Jessica Huntley, of Bogle-L'Ouverture, the first Black publishers in Britain, as she performed her poems in celebration of Black history month.

Asher sees performance poetry as "an opportunity to use every part of my body to express my experiences as a black woman. The poetry is lifted off the page and moves around. It moves with your body, with expression. There'll be times when I'm moving my hips, tapping my feet, nodding my head, moving my arms around. I find reading some poetry very difficult and it takes the pleasure away, but performing poetry can help you understand it more easily. You're very vulnerable, however, as a performance poet. You're there with your own material that you've written yourself. It's not acting, a play, a production, where you're pretending to be something you're not. It's a very responsible position. I'm a nervous person who's learnt to be courageous!"

As regards publishing, Asher says: "People have asked me if they can buy my book and I have to say that I have no book yet, but if you want a particular poem I will send you a copy. If I was ever to publish, I would like people to hear the poems as well, so they can understand them better, so they can hear the rhythm, whether it's a rap or a song or a chat."

Her favourite poets are Benjamin Zephaniah, Linton Kwesi Johnson and Jean 'Binta' Breeze, because their poetry is "accessible and reminds me of reggae". Linton Kwesi Johnson was speaking for the younger generation who were suffering from such low expectations in school. While he was commenting on the Brixton riots, Asher saw parts of Chapeltown burnt down.

She likes Maya Angelou, too, because she presents herself confidently as a big woman and is a positive role model. In 'Phenomenal Woman', for example, she writes of herself as a strong Black woman:

> Pretty women wonder where my secret lies.
> I'm not cute or built to suit a fashion model's size
> But when I start to tell them,
> They think I'm telling lies.
> I say,
> It's in the reach of my arms,
> The span of my hips,
> The stride of my step,
> The curl of my lips.
> I'm a woman

> Phenomenally.
> Phenomenal woman,
> That's me.

One of her favourite poems is Shelley's 'Mask of Anarchy', about the massacre of demonstrators at Peterloo, Manchester, in 1819, which begins:

> As I lay asleep in Italy
> There came a voice from over the Sea,
> And with great power it forth led me
> To walk in the visions of Poesy.

She likes the poem because it talks about oppression and exploitation, but also, as Bob Marley says, about a small axe cutting down a big tree, as the chorus goes:

> Rise like Lions after slumber
> In unvanquishable number,
> Shake your chains to earth like dew
> Which in sleep had fallen on you -
> Ye are many - they are few.

Some of the main themes of her own poetry are race, exploitation in the work-place, oppression and the plight of women. 'The Rebellious One', for example, begins:

> I am Africa steeped in sun
> I am where the story begun
> For I am the rebellious one
> Working the land
> And praying for freedom.

A poem about the work-place is called 'Bussing We Arse fe de Two Pennies' and starts:

> Don't expect silence
> Or the comfort of my smile

> For I can come rough and ready
> If you overstep de line
>
> Too much managers tekkin too much liberty wid we
> Dem no care too much bout we dignity
> Trampling down pan we sensibilities
> While we bussing we arse fe de two pennies.

As for writing her poems: "The first line is very important and sometimes takes a long time to come. But the time will come when it arrives, either in spurts when I can't get the pen to move quick enough, or piece by piece by piece till eventually it's there. A poem can come to me anywhere: on the street, at my desk, washing the dishes, doing housework. I do enjoy writing poetry."

She believes more could be done in schools to encourage a love of poetry: "You've got to be able to identify with it in some way. For some people it's just too complicated. And it's not always taught enthusiastically. It would help to have more poets in schools and get students to write their own poetry about whatever they want. They have to see the connection between what Shakespeare and Shelley were writing about and their own situation now. I wasn't allowed to study Shakespeare, but having seen several of his plays, including *King Lear* with Robert Stephens, I can now quote from him:

> The weight of this sad time we must obey;
> Speak what we feel, not what we ought to say.
> The oldest hath borne most: we that are young,
> Shall never see so much, nor live so long.

Asher runs poetry workshop sessions with students and her constant advice is: "Read as much as possible and listen to tapes of poetry. Go out and listen to performance poets. Have some faith in you own ability and in your own experience. It might not be the best poem ever written, but it will be a start!"

SECOND GENERATION STORY

I don't come from the Caribbean
Where the palm trees lean over the sea
I don't come from the Caribbean
Where you can feel soft sand underneath your feet
I don't come from the Caribbean
Where the mangoes them can so sweet
I don't come from the Caribbean
Where your skin can shine underneath the heat

So who will speak out for those
That are excluded
Who should have been included
Don't you see how some a crack
Deh pan de street a chat
Walking barefoot in the snow
Can no longer feel de cold

Don't you see how we a say
Look de man dem garn mad
But they are now casualties
And cannot mek a stand

Now some full a fear
An a so dem a react
Dem a carry de gun
Dem a carry de crack
You tink dem want mad
In a disya promise land

Where palm trees have been exchanged
For the changing colours of the leaves
On the chestnut tree
That stands overlooking the hustle and bustle
Of their constant struggle

Where the fruits of their labours

Are often bitter sweet
With the English cold
Getting in their bones
In a place some people say
We shouldn't call home

I don't come from the Caribbean
Where the palm trees lean over the sea
I don't come from the Caribbean
Where you can feel soft sand underneath your feet
I don't come from the Caribbean
Where the mangoes them can so sweet
I don't come from the Caribbean
Where your skin can shine underneath the heat

But it's only half a story till the other side is told
It's not all a we left out in de cold
It's a long time now we stop accept dem rejection
We done claim we rights
To live ya in a Englan
We nah wait for nobody
To gi we permission
We nah wait for nobody
To mek we feel welcome

We have we opinions
And we a put dem wid conviction
Some a hold up dem corner
Hold up dem position
Some out deh now a get a education
Some out deh now a become musician
Some a influence food
Influence fashion
Some a write poetry
Some a write novels

Plenty a we out deh
Have nuff ambition

We know it is a struggle
We struggle to survive
But we won't forget de casualties
They were left behind

Second generation
Born in a Englan
Never got de chance to put their opinion
Never got de chance to really mek a difference

I don't come from the Caribbean
Where the palm trees lean over the sea
I don't come from the Caribbean
Where you can feel soft sand underneath your feet
I don't come from the Caribbean
Where the mangoes them so sweet
I don't come from the Caribbean
Where your skin can shine underneath the heat.

TALKING BOOK

Reading a book is a political act
I wish someone had've told me that
I wish I had've known of the sacrifices made
So that I could simply sit, turn the page

It's only now that I am mature in age
I look back at those mundane days
Sitting in classrooms bored out of my brains
I'm listening to teachers express in such an
unexpressive way
The tiny words written on the academic page
That if understood would get me a job some day

Some day I won't need this place
Reading will take second place
I don't need words to conquer me
I will learn all I need from the streets
Till the streets taught me
That nothing in life is free
That every freedom that I have
Is earnt politically

Even the freedom of being able to read
Someone fought for that for me
So let us come together
Let us check out history
For the reality me a deal with
Is slavery

Now William Wells Brown
He knows what I mean
He wanted to read so bad
He couldn't even sleep
He used to bribe the white street children
With a lick of his sweet
Coz he knew being able to read

Would mean power, you see

See-saw, Marjorie Daw
Check out the man
Dem call him Gronniosaw

Now he, my friends
Was an African prince
Captured as a slave
Sailed on the slave ship
Observed his master reading to his crew
Decided he would like to do that too
But when he raised the book up to his ear
It never made a sound
So he went in search to find out
Where the secret could be found

What was the difference
Between the master and he
Why did not words jump out and speak
Maybe those words
Maybe they despise me

Can't you see how that's important
Can't you see how that is deep
I don't need no more than that
To try and convince me

That reading a book is a political act
I wish someone had've told me that
I wish I had've known of the sacrifices made
So that I could simply sit, turn the page.

GET UP STAN UP

Get up stan up
A your time now woman
Let the breeze touch your face
Let the world embrace you woman

You never let the wind blow you down
You never let the rain mek you drown
Experience is a ting why
You'll always be around now woman

Look how long you have been steering that ship
You make it look like there is nothing to it
But only you can give it credit now woman

So come out a de winter
An enter into spring
Coz dat is de time
When nature's nurturing
No badda mek de wickedness
Get into your runnins now woman

Always look forward
Never look back
Know that from time
That you've been held back
But what's in the heart
Can't be bought with cash
So put away the stash
You don't need to prove
Yourself to any man

Get up stan up
For a your time now woman
Let the breeze touch your face
Let the world embrace you woman.

ADISA

Adisa was born in 1968 in Poplar in the East End of London, but after a year, his family left and moved to Luton, in Bedfordshire. His father was a strict disciplinarian, but he had a good upbringing, with a strong family background, which included two elder brothers. His mother was the one who handed down his Caribbean culture.

He enjoyed going to primary school, but began to lose interest in secondary school, finding it difficult to see the relationship between school and the outside world: "I would be studying something like algebra and think I'm not going to use this and the teachers weren't on the level where they could show me the connection. I know there is a connection there between maths and the outside world. So I was just dropping back, just cruising, and by the time I got to my fifth year, I didn't want to do the exams. I thought I'd just leave and get a job."

His favourite subjects at school were English and Drama, and also PE because he played rugby for many years and really enjoyed it: "I liked English because of reading plays like *Oliver* which was a great inspiration. I loved Drama, taking a role and being a character. That was brilliant for me. I'll always remember that. That interest in Drama was always there, but was never really nurtured in my younger days. It lay dormant till I was about 25 when I started doing poetry. I also loved writing my own stories. I thought I was good at creative writing."

Adisa also liked Home Economics, mainly because he had a crush on the cookery teacher: "I enjoyed cooking as a child. I used to cook my own food at home. The teacher was very good - she looked after me. I was getting into trouble a lot at school, mucking around and talking, nothing major, and she was there to help me back on track. She said I should have become a chef and I took it seriously. I did my work experience at a hospital, in the kitchen, gearing up to be a chef, and then she left before the end of my time, so I kind of lost the plot."

His interest in poetry started at the age of 21 when he joined a sound system called Sovereign Roadshow: "The main DJ was Crucial Robbie and I was his apprentice. He made this well-known record called *Proud to be Black* and it was really cool to be in this sound system, Luton's finest. I was an MC and wrote rhymes about everything from girls to Jamaica, though I'd never been there. I was from Montserrat. This was my first experience of writing rhymes. I didn't see it as poetry at all - far from it."

In 1991, Adisa moved back to London and started becoming a bit more aware of himself as a Black person: "I wasn't into reading at school. Someone gave me a book of Malcolm X's last speeches. The only reason I read it was that I had started listening to hip hop and Public Enemy were talking about reading Malcolm X. So I read it and became inspired by him. I wanted to talk to people about him and write poems. I was getting upset about a lot of things - I was in my angry phase. I stopped the sound system stuff and started writing poetry, to deal with my emotions that way."

He read out his first poem in a Black history meeting in Tottenham, organised by the Pan-African Congress Movement: "Every now and then at the Marcus Garvey history club I would read a poem. It wasn't really a performance, more of a sharing. My first real performance was at Chat's Palace in Hackney, where there used to be regular poetry readings. You go along and do the 'open mike'. I always read with my big folder with my poems in there neatly. I used to read the words quite stiffly. I was quite passionate about them, but there was no drama. It wasn't coming alive. I remember shaking. It wasn't that I was scared, but it was like the energy of the poem was moving through me. It was so powerful and meant so much to me. Afterwards, it was nice because people would say they really enjoyed it. It was a very supportive environment."

One of his earliest poems was called 'Where's Your Head?':

> Head off the notion to be too head strong
> Headhunters' baskets are full of Heads
> Who did not heed this song

Headless people walk in circles
Unaware, these panicking chickens are already dead
Baskets full of aching heads,
Worrying over what's been done and said
Headteacher is your guide to success,
If you're willing to be led
You see!
Head teacher dwells in the place you call your Head.

For Adisa, performance poetry means "making it come alive, with tone, facial expression, body movement - being able to connect with your audience, making the space one, bouncing off people and interacting. It's dynamic, not just that I've got something to tell you and you're going to sit there and be quiet and take it in."

He has recently been thinking about publishing his poetry, particularly a book of poetry for children who are his main audience. He has performed in over 300 schools: "In primary schools they generally like poetry, but in secondary schools their initial reaction is to think that poetry is boring, so I know I have a challenge every single time. But when I start, they switch on to it. It's the energy and performance that turn them around - the conviction and passion.

"Poetry is unpopular in secondary schools because the students don't see its relevance. One way round this would be to take in to a workshop the latest Eminem song and show the poetry structure that is in it, show that whether it's rap or song, it's all coming from the same tree. Relevance, that's the key. Using poetry about issues that affect them – they're going through puberty, girls, boys, whatever - let them write about things like that. Then introduce them to the big stuff, rather than the other way round. The person teaching it also has to show passion."

Adisa's favourite poets are Langston Hughes, Maya Angelou, Linton Kwesi Johnson, Roger McGough, William Blake and Mutabaruka. His favourite poems are Maya Angelou's 'Still I Rise' and Langston Hughes's 'Harlem (2)':

What happens to a dream deferred?

Does it dry up
Like a raisin in the sun?

Or fester like a sore –
And then run?
Does it stink like rotten meat?
Or crust and sugar over –
Like a syrupy sweet?

Maybe it just sags
like a heavy load.

Or does it explode?

He also wishes he had written Benjamin Zephaniah's 'White Comedy' which begins:

I waz whitemailed
By a white witch,
Wid white magic
An white lies,
Branded a white sheep
I slaved as a whitesmith
Near a white spot
Where I suffered whitewater fever.

People who have influenced him are mainly musicians and singers, as he experienced them first, before poets - James Brown, Gil Scott-Heron, Aretha Franklin, Curtis Mayfield, Bob Marley.

Adisa used to write his poetry at any time, for example waking up in the middle of the night with an idea. Now he tends to sit down at his desk, write down an idea and then try and work with it: "I love it, but it's a job, so I have to discipline myself and say it's time to work now." His inspiration often comes from observation: "I observe situations, like on the tube or in a club, watching dramas unfold."

The themes of his poetry are "birth and life, being optimistic, tying things to the Black experience and linking them back to the Caribbean and our culture", like his poem 'Teddy Bear':

My Teddy Bear's got dreadlocks
Right down to the middle of his back,

Each spiralling like a corkscrew,
Tight springs painted black.

He advises young poets: "Read every day, read as much as you can, increase your vocabulary and write every day. Try different styles, comedy, poetry from India and Africa, be diverse."

WHAT IS POETRY?

Poetry is everywhere
Poetry is music to your ear
Poetry is a graceful dancer with elegance and flair
Poetry has many shapes and forms, but poetry is not
     square
Poetry is written on paper, but poetry doesn't live
     there
For poetry is in your eyes, in your smile and even in
     your tears
Poetry is your happiness, your anger and also your
     fear

Poetry is in the way you walk
Some folks walk around as if they're barmy
Some folks walk like they're in the army
Some people walk as slow as a snail
Some people walk like they have four legs and a tail

Poetry is an African drum playing a heartbeat
Poetry is the cold wind that blows and the sun that
     gives us heat
Poetry is dad's old boots and dad's cheesy feet
Poetry wakes me in the morning and closes my eyes
     at night to sleep
Poetry is a plate of fresh vegetables because I don't
     eat meat

Poetry is rhythm that goes on and on and on......
Poetry is Bob Marley singing my favourite song
Buffalo soldier, dreadlock Rasta

Poetry lives and poetry cannot die
Poetry is Imagination
If you want to, you can touch the sky
Poetry is the sound of a newborn baby
When it begins to cry

Mamaaaaaaaaaaa!
Poetry needs to be read, like a bird needs to fly
So when I ask the question
'What is poetry?'
You should all be very clear
Because 'Poetry is everywhere.'

MAMMA ALWAYS TOLD ME

Mamma always told me
Son, walk the streets with your head held high
You have no limitations, if you want to you can fly
Success does not come to those who sit down and wait
If you don't knock, no one will open the gate

Mamma always told me
Put God first in everything you do
Believe in yourself and your dreams will come true
Some will try to hold you down
Never regret your skin is brown

Mamma always told me
The road of life is rough and oh so long
When you fall down, pick yourself up and carry on
Respect your parents and elders, so your days may
    be long
When you have your children, sing to them this song

Mamma always told me
If you play with puppy, one day dog lick your mouth
No matter how hard the problem, you can work it out

Mamma always told me
Put a little by for a rainy day
Remember what you sew shall be your pay
There's a time to work and a time to play
Bend the tree while it's young, so when it's older it
    won't go astray

Mamma always told me
When turkey foot broke, it keep company with fowl
Try to see everything around you, just like the owl

Mamma always told me
You never miss the water till the well run dry

Because you're a man, it doesn't mean you can't cry
In the classroom of life, don't be afraid to ask
WHY
There is no such thing as failure
As long as you make up your mind to try

Mamma always told me
There are two sides to every story
But!
Until the lions tell their story, the hunter will always
  get the glory

Mamma always told me
A pickney who doesn't heed to their mother
Will have to drink pepper, lime juice and salt
You will be judged not by your words
But by the content of your heart

Mamma always told me
Everybody has their own cross to bear
Look them in the eye, show them no fear
If a job is worth doing, it's worth doing right
Truth will always triumph over might
From the darkness must come the light

CHICK PEA PIE

In the food bacchanal
Food just a jam to the steel pan
No humans in sight
Strictly vegetables deh pon the street
Tonight

I see rice a jump high
Somersaulting in the wind
Kidney peas too fat to jump
Her belly just a drag pon the floor

Chick peas swimming in an ocean of curry
Plantain a sunbathe, skin turn black in the sun
Green banana making eyes
At chocho
Him say tonight I must get that one

Aubergine a whine she waist
Putting a smile on
Dasheen and yam face
Two bad bwoys
Who never skin teeth
When them see aubergine
They ball, what a girl look sweet

Spinach and cousin callaloo
A try fe tease black-eye peas
Spinach flutter her eyelashes
Black-eye body start to swell
Callaloo blow peas a kiss
I think I am in love
Peas start fe YELL

Okra a chat to
Big belly breadfruit
About the good old years

That passed them by
Breadfruit rub him charcoal belly
And lift him head to the sky
Okra skin is no longer furry
Her insides are scaly and dry

What has become of our youth?
How fast life has passed us by
Observing the others next to them
Aubergine, plantain and yam
Tears swelled up in their eyes
For tonight after the carnival
They would all surely die
For tomorrow mamma will cook them
In her famous
                                                    Chick Pea Pie.

CUBAN REDD

Cuban Redd is the performance name for Shirley E. Mason. She chose it partly as a tribute to her mother who comes from Cuba. Her father is Jamaican and Shirley herself was born in Kingston. She does not really remember anything about Jamaica, however, as she came to England when she was only three years old.

At infant school she remembers learning to tell the time: "One day I was looking at the clock above the door leading to the playground and it was like a revelation. All of a sudden it made complete sense to me and I could tell the time." She also recollects other children laughing at her because of her Jamaican accent: "We were doing nursery rhymes in class. My nursery rhyme was –

> Rain ah fall
> Breeze ah blow
> Chicken batty
> Out ah door

"They all started laughing and I was told it was wrong because they were reciting Jack and Jill and Baa Baa Black Sheep. It was nothing like the rhythm or the feel of what I was doing. They didn't understand what I was doing. I was doing it in very broad Jamaican. That hurt. I remember that hurting. It made me feel isolated and different."

Her favourite subject at school was English. She liked reading and writing stories: "At the end of primary school, I remember the teacher had been reading *A Tale of Two Cities* to us throughout the year, and on the last day she hadn't quite finished the story. So I stayed behind to clear up, sweep up, put up the chairs, just because I wanted to know what happened at the end of the story."

The reason she thinks poetry is often unpopular in school is that it is "still perceived as dry, on the page, dealing with subjects that are not relevant to young people. They still have the idea of 'I wandered lonely as a cloud' and don't realise the power that is in poetry. I think there is a change happening, however, with poets going into schools and reading or performing or facilitating workshops. This is changing the way that poetry is seen nowadays."

She now lives in Enfield and works in the local schools: "I tour with a theatre company called Face Front, writing the poetry to movement for the plays. The schools often ask me back just as a performance poet. I might perform at an assembly and then the students ask me questions, or I run a workshop. It's great to see them come alive, writing about what they're feeling inside, catching the rhythm, realising you can dance to poetry, that it's alive, that it can move you. Poetry needs to be vibrant, about what's happening around us or about something that you pull out that everyone experiences and can relate to."

Shirley started writing about her feelings and particular incidents when she was ten years old, often influenced by the bible, but she did not really start writing poems until she was 25. She was then a member of a Pentecostal church and she used to write religious poems which she would recite in church. One of them began:

> My life was in darkness
> My soul was in shame
> My body unconscious...

In 1996, she entered a poetry competition with 'Karma' and felt sure she was going to win – which she did! Someone saw her and asked her to perform some of her poems at Centreprise, in Hackney, and that is when she started out on the performance poetry scene: "At that time there weren't many black poets around and there weren't many women. I used to do gigs where there were a load of white men and me! So I started up my own club, called Dennawadis, to have more women and black performers. We also had singing groups, comedians and dancers."

Since then, Shirley has performed at many venues, including

Express Excess, Hackney Empire, Maidstone Prison, the Edinburgh Festival and Hay-on-Wye. In her view, performance poetry is something that lives: "During a performance the poetry will reach out, touch, change, make aware and open up. It will release and inform, make you laugh, dance and move. I want to be funny and make people laugh, but on the whole my poetry's very serious. It's about real things, not ethereal things; it's about real personal, historical things. Performing is not just standing up and saying words. It's how you look, your image, the way you act, the vibration. The people have paid to come and see you. You have to give them the best you can."

People have often asked her if she has published her poems and she used to say, "I need time to edit." But now she says: "I would like to be published, to have a wider audience, to leave something to posterity and show that negative cycles can be broken."

Her favourite poet is Maya Angelou and she likes reading her life and poetry together: "Just to talk about her makes me go shivery inside!" She enjoys Keats, Donne and George Herbert whom she studied for 'O' level, and she admires Jean 'Binta' Breeze. Among performance poets she also loves Adisa because he has such presence on the stage. Lemn Sissay influenced her in a workshop for Black poets and her favourite poem is Maya Angelou's 'Phenomenal Woman' which ends:

> Now you understand
> Just why my head's not bowed.
> I don't shout or jump about
> Or have to talk real loud.
> When you see me passing,
> It ought to make you proud.
> I say,
> It's in the click of my heels,
> The bend of my hair,
> The palm of my hand,
> The need for my care.
> 'Cause I'm a woman
> Phenomenally.
> Phenomenal woman,
> That's me.

Poetry can come to Shirley at any time: "For example, I might be in the kitchen washing up. I have pens and paper everywhere, including by my bedside. I just scribble a line or a thought at any time, or I put down the title of a poem and maybe something will come from it later. A poem I wrote about rape started with two lines in my head –

> When reality bites
> Then you must escape

"Then the poem just came." At other times, a poem might be more consciously 'crafted', like 'Poetic Therapy' which begins:

> The cracked contorted scream
> Hangs naked
> Shivering in the comfortless cold air.

Her inspiration can come from anywhere, including television, which, for instance, led to her writing about the massacre of schoolchildren at Dunblane in a poem called 'Five... Six', that begins:

> In primary schools, at English time,
> The children often said this rhyme:
> 1.. 2.. buckle my shoe
> 3.. 4.. knock at the door
> 5.. 6.. pick up sticks.
>
> That Day they stuck at five and six
> Sixteen will never pick up sticks.
> For that Day in Scottish School Dunblane
> Thomas Hamilton flipped..... INSANE.
> A church-going loner, self-confessed.
> Who would have known? Who would have guessed?
> That Day he'd vent his fearsome rage –
> And shoot to kill – on wild rampage.
> By bursting into Dunblane School
> He disregarded every rule.

Some of the themes of her poetry are romance, inspiration, coming through difficult times, homelessness, honesty. In a poem called 'Lies' she writes:

>Lies are used to dominate
>Lies replace sweet love with hate
>Lies used to manipulate
>Will crush your very soul
>
>Lies are proud and cheating
>Lies encourage beatings
>But Truth creates a meeting
>In a place that's whole.

Her advice to young poets is: "Write from the heart - what you really feel. Don't pretend. It's got to speak of you. See what's going on in performance poetry. Get inspired and challenged. Don't get complacent. Be grounded in the physical reality of everyday life, while simultaneously reaching to 'hang out' in the stars."

KARMA (TRIBUTE AND ENCOURAGEMENT TO MY PEOPLE)

Soon....
Soon....
Soon.

Rear Rear Rear Rear Rear
Dat's all dem ah seh every deah
Dem stan up annah chat
Annah chew dem fat
Soon dem ah have fe go peah

They say that we come from the monkey
And how we all smell very funky
Still they stole us from our shores chained line by line
To serve them and praise them and KISS their behind
Dividing our families, destroying our lives
Using our men and raping our wives
Battered and beaten by whips on our backs
Yet feeding us JESUS to avert our attacks

Rear Rear Rear Rear Rear
Soon dem ah have fe go peah

They rumoured that the streets here were paved
    with Gold
We came in our thousands, unwarned of the cold
They pinned notes on the door to scream loud and
    shout
No Irish, No Dogs, NO BLACKS... KEEP OUT

Rear Rear Rear Rear Rear
Soon dem ah have fe go peah

The rooms that we did find we all had to share
Sometimes with laughter and sometimes with fear
Huddled together round paraffin lamps

Grateful for company, ignoring the damp
Slaving in hospitals, trains and on buses
We bought boots, coats, gloves and yes, even houses
Though they raised up petitions to hinder the sale
We purchased our properties, we did not fail

So now, it's the millennium!.. and we have arrived
Have we learnt from our 'STORY', what have we
　　　derived?
Are we still divided, still being ruled
Still being SAMBO'D and playing the fool-fool?
Let's look to our future, direct our own fate
Keep learning our STORY, don't leave it too late
Be healed and united, reclaiming our past
Rise up – and be counted, it's time to stand fast

Rear Rear Rear Rear Rear
Soon dem ah have fe go peah

Soon....
Soon....
Soon.

TALKING, TALKING, TALKING (FOR ANGELA)

Talking, Talking, Talking
Saying, doing nothing
But kicking up a storm
Of warm, stale fetid air
    You really do not care

If you cared
About the black man's fight
The homeless white
That vacant abused child
That's running wild
And turning tricks
With everyone he meets
Along drug-sodden streets
You would do more
Than

Talking, Talking, Talking
Saying, doing nothing
But kicking up a storm
Of warm, stale, fetid air
    You really do not care

If you cared
About that man with Sickle Cell disease
That woman who can only squeeze
Just one more meal
So that her kids will feel full
One last time
Before she ends the fight
By killing her, and them, that night
You would do more
Than

Talking, Talking, Talking
Saying, doing nothing

But kicking up a storm
Of warm, stale, fetid air
      You really do not care

If you cared
You would change your stagnant life
Stop!... beating on your wife
You would save that threatened tree
That's stood majestically
Through moments, days and years
Of centuries' scenes unfurled
You'd protect our dying world
If you cared, if you cared
You would do more
Than

Talking, Talking, Talking
Saying, doing nothing
But kicking up a storm
Of warm, stale, fetid air
      Do we really care?

NO LIMIT

no limit, no limit
no limit, no limit

no limit for my sister
no limit for my brother
no limit for my people
for we're helping one another
we're slowly moving forward
we're running in the race
we're holding tight the baton
and we're picking up the pace
so don't you dis me sister
brother don't you raise a hand
let's lift up one another
in this cold cloudy land
let's educate our children
our princes and princesses
teach them how to be strong
and to build on our successes

no limit, no limit
no limit, no limit

no limit for the african
no limit for the jew
no limit for the protestant
the irish catholic too
no limit for the woman
no limit for the man
no limit for the child
as we unite across the land
we're taking back our future
we're gaining stolen ground
they turned the tables on us
but we are turning them around
we're rising like the phoenix

from the ashes of oppression
to soar with hungry wings
we're making no concessions

no limit, no limit
no limit, no limit

we'll work to stamp out racism
with dialogue persistent
like in the Stephen Lawrence case
we're coming strong, consistent
scottish, welsh or irish
english, black or white
we can create a balanced harmony
if we would just unite
to furnish strong foundations
of trust, basic respect
move with forgiveness to the future
(though we never will forget!)
politicians working hand in hand
with dancers, poets, healers
to break through all the barriers
to cut away concealers

all this is very possible
for you and you and me
when we begin within ourselves
to liberate, be free
starting at the root foundation
advancing to the crown
no limit is the battle cry
deliverance is the sound

no limit, no limit
no limit, no limit
no limit, no limit
nooooh limit!

LEVI TAFARI

Levi Tafari was born in Liverpool on 24 June, 1960. His parents came from Jamaica and brought him up strictly in Jamaican culture, as he remembers: "There were a lot of Caribbean and African people around. Liverpool has one of the oldest continuous black communities in Europe, because of the docks and the slave trade. I used to speak with a strong Jamaican accent because that's all I was hearing. The family that baby-sat me when my mum and dad went to work were also Jamaican. My mum is a great storyteller from the oral tradition, rich in culture and self-esteem."

As a family, with his sister Sheila and brother George, they used to travel around the country a lot: "I had an auntie in Birmingham and family in Manchester and dad had a brother in Bradford. Also, my parents worked very hard and managed to buy their own house. Liverpool was the place to be in the Sixties, with the Beatles. It was very popular." It also produced the Liverpool poets, Adrian Henri, Roger McGough and Brian Patten, who performed their poetry and published it together in a Penguin book entitled *The Mersey Beat*.

When he was five, he went to Granby Street Primary School: "The teachers couldn't understand me when I spoke, so they put me in a special class to speak English, along with Somali, Chinese and Indian children. I remember reading from a book, one time, and I had to read out the word 'enamel'. I said 'enam-ell' and the teacher made me say it several times in the English way."

He went to Arundel Comprehensive School where there was a high percentage of Black students, including a couple of his cousins. During the first few years, he did very little work, but eventually passed some CSEs: "My favourite subject was Art. I also like Technical Drawing and PE. I was good at basketball and ended up playing for Liverpool schoolboys. We used to go to Anfield to train, but this was the time of the skinheads and they'd be waiting. No one could guarantee my safety, so I stopped going."

One of his later poems expresses his view of the school curriculum:

> TING-A-LING-A-LING
> another bell ring
> dis is de ting dat
> dem teachin
> Christopher Columbus
> Sir Francis Drake
> and Henry de eighth
> 'but wait
> a nuh de man dat
> did dead from
> disease
> then is wha type
> a ting dat yuh
> a teach to mi
> wi want Haile Selassie
> Marcus Garvey
> Mary Seacole
> yes people like dat
> Martin Luther King
> and Malcolm X'
> 'Shut up!'
> de teacha seh mi
> too outa order and
> get well vex.

He did not like poetry at school: "It was mainly war poetry which I found boring. But I used to love nursery rhymes." One of his poems reflects this liking:

> PAT-A-CAKE, PAT-A-CAKE
> Bakers man
> I'll bake you a cake as fast as I can
> I'll put in some sugar
> I'll put in some rum
> Cause we want the people them to have some fun!

Levi believes that poetry used to be very unpopular in schools: "The poetry that was done wasn't relevant, the language was difficult, the rhythm difficult, the poets were dead two or three hundred years ago!"

His teachers wanted him to be a PE teacher, but he said to the head teacher that he wanted to travel: "She was a good head teacher. She was a socialist and very fair. If you got into trouble with a teacher, she'd take both of you aside and talk to you both. She was cool. She suggested I do catering and I said that sounded good. So I went to Colquitt Street Catering College, got a distinction and went into the industry."

He first started writing poems at the age of sixteen. One of his earliest was about slavery:

> Tribulation
> Sufferation
> Things well known by the black population
> Some crying
> Some dying
> Some fighting for a solution
> Taken away by force from home
> Brought down here
> To slave in Rome
> Brutality we had never known
> Until they took us from our home.

He has been influenced by the Black Power movement in the United States, by writers such as George Jackson, Angela Davis and Stokely Carmichael, and describes the themes of his poetry as "Rastafarianism, Babylon system, black pride, the environment, social and political issues."

The first performance Levi did was at Chaucer's nightclub in

Liverpool city centre in September, 1981, just after the riots. There was a BBC film crew there for another purpose, but they filmed his performance, too, and his poem 'Nuh Blame Rasta' was televised. It begins:

> The riots in a Liverpool
> Who is to blame?
> Please don't call the RASTAMANS name
> Peace and love is the RASTAMANS aim
> Suh rioting is not the RASTAMANS game
>
> The riots in a Liverpool nuh blame RASTA
> Oppression and injustice could never prosper
> All over England is a total disaster
> The burning and the looting nuh blame RASTA.

At this time, he also decided, on the advice of a friend, to join the Liverpool 8 Writers Workshop: "I refused to go at first. I thought, 'I don't want to go to no workshop. They're going to criticise my writing and tell me I can't write'. But eventually I decided to go and it was really good. They liked my work. The South African poet and playwright David Evans was involved with the group and he really encouraged me. So too did Olive Rogers and the Jamaican poet Ken Chevannes." At this time, Levi was still a chef, but in 1983 he left catering when his wife Carol was pregnant with their son Ezekiel.

Levi sees performance poetry as "taking poetry off the page and bringing it alive, keeping the oral tradition alive. It's a function of the heart. This is why rap is so popular – rhythmically applied poetry – the griot tradition which has survived the Middle Passage, the griot being the traditional consciousness-raiser, storyteller, newscaster and political agitator. It's performance poetry that has made poetry as popular as it is today. It's a mission not a competition."

He has teamed up with reggae, soul and funk fusion bands, most notably The Ministry of Love, and has worked with Delado, the African Drum and Dance Ensemble. He also spent some time with Mohammad Khalil as poets in residence with the Royal Liverpool Philharmonic Orchestra. He has performed his poetry all over the world; in 1992, he appeared as himself in Grange Hill; and in 1996, he went to Ethiopia to make a BBC film on Rastafarianism, entitled 'From Babylon to Zion'. Levi also works in education - running creative writing workshops in schools, colleges, universities, youth centres, prisons and libraries.

As for publishing his poetry, he says: "Society puts the emphasis on publication. To me it's good, but I prefer to perform and keep it live and keep it real. Books are good for those you can't reach, but not everybody can read, so people need to hear as well." At present, he is preparing his fourth book of poems, entitled 'Rap in Paper'.

Among his favourite poets are Louise Bennett, Maya Angelou, Benjamin Zephaniah, Mohammad Khalil, Mutabaruka and Oku Onuora. His all-time favourite, however, is Mikey Smith and, in particular, his poem 'Me Cyaan Believe It'. He also likes Mikey Smith's 'I An I Alone', which begins:

> I an I alone
> a trod through creation.
> Babylon on I right, Babylon on I lef,
> Babylon in front of I an Babylon behind I,
> an I an I alone in the middle
> like a Goliath wid a sling-shot.
>
> 'Ten cent a bundle fi me calaloo!
> Yuh a buy calaloo, dread? Ten cent.'
>
> Everybody a try fi sell someting,
> everybody a try fi grab someting,
> everybody a try fi hustle someting,
> everybody a try fi kill someting,
>
> but ting an ting mus ring,
> an only a few can sing
> cause dem naw face de same sinting.

When Mikey Smith was killed on Stony Hill, Levi wrote a poem which ends with the chorus:

> Dem a murdera
> Dem a murdera
> Dem kill Michael Smith
> Inna Jamaica
> Who do it
> Who kill I an I dub poet
> Yes wi warn answer
> Yes wi warn answer
> Cause tings like dis
> Carn't guh nuh furtha
> Suh who do it, who do it
> Who kill Michael Smith
> Who kill Michael Smith
> 'Mad house… Mad house… Mad house
> Mi seh mi c-yaan believe it.'

Levi says the influences on his poetry have come, not mainly from other poets, but from Jamaican DJs like Big Youth and U-Roy, the sound systems and from Bob Marley, as in 'Redemption Song':

> Emancipate yourselves from mental slavery
> None but ourselves can free our minds.

He describes the way he writes: "I get an idea and just keep going over it in my head and then eventually I get around to writing it down. I don't like working on a computer. I like to write long-hand and then type it up on the computer. That way you can see what you've crossed out and how it's developed. I write when the inspiration takes me, unless it's a commission and you have to produce it within a particular time, like when Granada wanted me to write a poem about the release of Nelson Mandela. I find that easier in a way, because you're under pressure and you have to do it!"

His advice to anyone beginning to write poetry is: "Be true to yourself. Research what you're writing about. Try not to be too selfish, because the oral tradition is a communal system. It's not one person up there, like America's motto 'One out of many'. Ours is more a Jamaican motto, 'Out of many, one people'. Be prepared to work hard and be sincere."

DE TONGUE (DE FIRST INSTRUMENT)

De tongue
was de very first instrument
When it was played
it caused a lot of excitement
Now it can be played good or bad
de sounds can be bubbly
or be sad
It has been known
to tell de truth
den agen de tongue
can lie like a brute

If yuh lie wid yuh tongue
it will get yuh inna muddle
and yuh will get trouble
pon de double
Nuh bother trouble, trouble
weh nuh trouble yuh

I play I tongue
to project de truth
and hope I can
inspire de youths
I wish I could play
Drums, bass and flute
den I could be a one man group
But it sticks wid I
night and day
most of de time yuh can hear it play

BUM CHA BUM A BUM CHA
BUM CHA BUM A BUM BUM CHA
BUM CHA BUM A BUM CHA
BUM CHA BUM A BUM BUM CHA

It can be polite

and it can be rude
But what is unique
about dis instrument
is it can also taste FOOD

MY VOCATION

When I left school at sixteen
I had done the best I could
because I wanted a profession
that would do me good
Well I didn't enlist in the army
because I was already tough
and I couldn't be a professor
you see I was not mad enough
No chance of being a politician
organized crime is not for me
plus the sight of blood made me squeamish
so a doctor I could not be
Got to get a profession
which will be around a real long time
so I got involved in poetry
Oh! The security of rhyme
So one day I visited a job agency
to explain what I wanted to do
the woman looked at me very strange
and asked me if I'd been sniffing glue
"Well you'll have to do an apprenticeship
just like any other profession."
"Go to the park and check it out
it's full of inspiration."
"Study the park carefully
see it in all its grandeur."
I thought she said, "If you go to the park
we'll give you some ganga."
Ben Johnson couldn't have caught me
I got down there really fast
But all the signs left me bewildered
They all said, "PLEASE KEEP OFF THE GRASS!"

THE FIRST WOMAN IN MY LIFE

A woman's work is never done
If you don't believe me ask my mum
She worked her fingers to the bone
to provide us with a decent home
if she lived in Ancient Rome
She could have built that city on her own
She cooks, she cleans
She does everything
She irons, decorate and does the shopping
She chastised us when we were rude
but never sent us to bed without food
Every day she would change our clothes
if we had colds she would wipe our nose
or if we went to her with a problem
mum would do her best to solve them
We didn't want for anything
We got the greatest gift her lovin
You can have ten aunties
and scores of lovers
but remember you only have one mother
I remember someone called me a nigger
mum says you're Black, beautiful and you have a
culture
She always made sure we went to school
cause in this life you can't be a fool
you see people will ride you like a mule
It was mum who taught me to be cool
Mother there's something you should know
I love you, I love you, I love you so
you taught me to survive in the ghetto
yes you can have my last ROLLO
if it wasn't for you I wouldn't exist
So here it comes for you a kiss
Yes you was the first woman in my life
but one day I will take a wife
Then like you she will become a mum
A woman's work is never done.

NO DISGRACE

Monkeys don't live in brick houses
fishes don't have knees
Women don't have hairs on their chest
and men can't have babies
Crocodiles cannot fly
and parrots don't swim
You see second place
is no real disgrace
it's not all the time you will win.

MELANIN

Melanin I love you
you mean so much to me
Oh! Melanin your beauty
is far richer than the eye can see
My Melanin embraces me
from my head down to my toe
Oh! Melanin I would never forsake you
this I want you to know.

You lie with me
when I sleep at night
You guide me
through the day
You take me to
a higher height
I love to watch
you at play.

I often face heavy abuse
when you're out with me
some people haven't got my Melanin
so they show their jealousy
But no matter what they say or do
it won't stop me from loving you
My Melanin
precious Melanin
the pigmentation in my skin.

BLACKROOTS INNA BABYLON

Spiritually rooted
Culturally aware
a mystical African atmosphere
a cultural beat on a African drum
like the beat of we heart
when life began
Blackman roots inna Babylon
a positive vibration
inna wicked land
a disciplined man
inna undisciplined land
a spiritual fight
a fight against wrong
art and craft combined together
music and dance
fe the brothers and sisters
Natural livin upon the earth
but inna Babylon
what is life really worth?

A concrete jungle
where it is cold
and a man could a
easily lose his soul
a place where the sun
it barely shines
and the smoking of herbs
is a crime
A technical place
full of machines
where a man is not
respected as a human being
if yuh have a black skin
them seh that is a sin
inna land a competition
black skin can't win.

Now the roots of Black culture
is here
suh Babylonians yuh better
tek care
cause we help build up your land
and now we want our share
suh give us a African atmosphere
give Black culture a chance
and let peace and love advance
cause we're coming out of the trance
an a guh straight inna African dance.

A cultural education
fe all Black youths
not a selfish education
fe mek them a brute
suh teach Black culture
in your schools
then the runnings
inna Babylon may be cool
because we're
Spiritually rooted
Culturally aware
and we want a cultural atmosphere
a cultural beat
inna African way
cause African culture
is with us to STAY.

PATIENCE AGBABI

Patience Agbabi was born in Paddington, London, on 26 August, 1965. She was fostered for sixteen years with a white English family during term-time and spent her school holidays in London with her Nigerian parents. She lived with her foster parents in rural Sussex and north Wales. She now lives in London, but still feels the urge to get to the countryside or seaside for some of the time.

There were some difficulties having two different sets of friends, but despite some contradictions, she now thinks it an advantage to have had access to two different cultures:

> but they held my nose and force
> fed me on two cultures
> egg and chips or eba and groundnut stew
>
> nothing got past the
> lump
> in my throat
>
> In Sussex they used to say
> 'You don't pronounce it like that
> in England... did you pick that up from your
>
> parents?' And in London
> 'Your cockney voice is so ugly

why can't you speak properly?'
('Serious Pepper')

Patience generally liked school: "I was quite good at school. I was able to learn things very easily, but by the time I took my 'O' Levels, I was starting to get a bit sick of school. Instead of learning for fun, it was all about getting your 'O' Levels. My parents put me under a lot of pressure. Doing 'A' Levels was a nice feeling, however, because it was more optional. Sixth form was the best because we had a lot of free lessons, time to bond with your mates and play lots of music. English was my favourite subject. I liked the novels and the poetry. I struggled a bit with Physics, but I liked French and German - the sounds of the different languages."

The poetry she read at school included Thom Gunn, Patrick Kavanagh, R. S. Thomas and her favourite, Ted Hughes, especially his animal poems. She also loved Dylan Thomas. For 'A' Level she studied *Macbeth* – "brilliant poetry, the best thing ever!"

Her advice for encouraging a love of poetry in school is: "Bring in as many poets as possible. The poetry's got to be live and it's good for the students to meet the poets. It makes it real, exciting and relevant. They get to hear it and ask questions. They should hear the poems first before they study them line by line."

Patience first started writing short stories when she was seven and by the age of thirteen she was writing lyrics, inspired by punk and 'two-tone' music: "It was the sort of stuff you wouldn't show your parents - sex, drugs and rock 'n' roll, lots of swear words, almost designed to shock, very gritty."

Her first performance was at Centreprise in Hackney where she was a member of a women's writing group: "We did readings every so often. I had written a prose piece about finding a flat in London. It was really humorous and it made people laugh. I thought, 'I like doing this. I must do more of this!'"

Give me a stage and I'll cut form on it
give me a page and I'll perform on it.
('Prologue')

The first poem she performed was in Kentish Town at an Apples and Snakes workshop which ended up with a performance: "It was a rap poem and people were screaming and stamping. That was the time I thought I am definitely going to perform my poetry. I got a lot of good feedback from established poets such as Ahmed Sheikh of African Dawn."

> Hip hop hip
> hyp hop
> hypnotic rap rhythm
> rocks from the lips
> of the slave ships
> The Griot grits images
> of skeleton villages
> and the Monkey sits Stackolee
> in the African American tree-top
> trying to outwit
> the king of the concrete jungle.
> ('Stings Like a Bee')

Since then, Patience has performed at many venues, from Glastonbury and the Royal Albert Hall, to tiny pubs and arts centres: "Performance poetry must be accessible, so that someone who is not into poetry, or even thinks they don't like poetry, will listen to it and actually understand something the first time they hear it. They won't feel baffled or stupid. It's important that it reaches ordinary people. The poetry absolutely comes alive. It's about sharing poetry with as wide an audience as possible. I think that rhyme is very important. The music of the poem is celebrated through the rhythm and the rhyme and they both help you to remember the poem."

She was once a member of the now disbanded Atomic Lip, a writers' collective with the aim of taking poetry from the page to the stage, and she has also appeared on Channel 4's Litpop series. Recently, she did a Poetry Society residency at the Flamin' Eight Tattoo studio in north London where some of her short poems were used as tattoos.

As for publishing her poetry, she says: "I love books, so I think it's important that the poetry I perform is published. I love having something tangible. My first book, *R. A. W.*, was made up of poems

I had performed and I was at first worried that the poetry might not work on the page. But then I thought that rap lyrics are printed and they work."

> Coz I'm rappin it up in a real tight squeeze
> I don't cross my I's I don't dot my t's
> Wordsworth Milton line them up
> an they're dead I am PA an I am rappin it up
> ('Rappin It Up')

After *R.A.W.* was published, she says: "For two years I wrote almost nothing and I was really depressed about it. It was fear of doing a second book and I forgot the joy of writing."

Patience often makes notes before writing her poems and by the time she is ready to compose a poem she has a lot of it in her head already. She also finds it very easy to learn poems.

Her inspiration sometimes comes from listening to the radio or watching the news and documentaries on television - particularly for her overtly political poems. She has recently been re-reading Chaucer and Shakespeare and is impressed by how they made their work accessible to ordinary people at the time. In her second book, *Transformatrix*, she has written a modern version of 'The Wife of Bath', entitled 'The Wife of Bafa', which begins:

> My name is Mrs Alice Ebi Bafa
> I come from Nigeria.
> I am very fine, isn't it.
> My next birthday I'll be twenty-nine.
> I'm business woman.
> Would you like to buy some cloth?
> I have all the latest styles from Lagos,
> Italian shoe and handbag to match,
> lace, linen and Dutch wax.
> I only buy the best
> and I travel first class.
>   Some say I have blood on my hands
> 'cause I like to paint my nails red
> but others call me femme fatale.

> My father had four wives
> so I've had five husbands.
> I cast a spell with my gap-toothed smile
> and my bottom power.
> Three were good and two were bad.

Some of her favourite poets are Kwame Dawes, Simon Armitage and Jackie Kay, with Carol Ann Duffy as her "ultimate favourite". Many poets have helped her. Those who have inspired her most are the Grenadian, Merle Collins, who wrote the introduction to her first book, and Benjamin Zephaniah: "He encouraged me to get published. To see him perform was a sheer delight. His energy is electric."

She is concerned that there are not more women on the performance poetry circuit: "It is partly because it involves travel and time away from the family that women are less likely to be out there performing. It is also quite competitive and women are generally less competitive. I am competitive - with myself. And I do look at what certain men have achieved and say, 'I can do that!'"

The main themes of her poetry are 'women, identity, the duality of existence, people going through change and growing up'.

> If only I could light up your smile like Oprah
> enrapture your soul like Queen Latifah,
> say a little prayer for you like Aretha,
> make your caged bird rise and sing like Maya.
> ('If')

She thinks aspiring poets should try to meet other poets and see live performances. They should also read widely and not remain isolated.

THE CHANGE

I remember everything vividly that Sunday
by its absence. It was the day that God,
like Father Christmas and the tooth fairy,
no longer existed. The church smelt musty
and I noticed Mrs Leadbetter's glass eye.
I remember lip synching the Lord's Prayer

and Amen after father murmured grace
for Sunday dinner. At the head of the table
sat a leg of lamb, more like a sacrifice
than a roast. Our golden Labrador, Petra,
sloped off into the sitting room, and hid.

Father carved while mother served raw carrots,
pureed swede and something resembling cabbage.
I can still taste it in the back of my throat.
The only sound was stainless steel on china

till I realised the potatoes were missing
and said it, and my mother turned, a blur
of plate spinning across the room and breaking.

My father said "She's going through The Change."
I stared into the kitchen floor and wondered

what, in God's name, she was changing into.

IT'S BETTER POST- THAN PRE-

I'm sitting on this toilet seat
I'm reading graffiti
and some of it's political
and some of it is cheeky
but I only see red
coz I'm feeling rather freaky
when it comes to having PMT
no woman can beat me
I'm speedy I'm angry
I'm horny I'm stoned
I want to be touched
and I WANNA BE LEFT ALONE
PMT I pick my target
PMT I start to load
PMT I pull my trigger
my tits are ready to explode

Stick em on stick em in stick em up gals
stick em on stick em in stick em up
if you wanna shoot an arrow
then it's time to load your barrel
stick em on stick em in stick em up

I remember that first memory
a dark red stain
I didn't feel no nausea
I didn't feel no pain
I was a woman a warrior
exotic arcane
and once a month a lunatic
in nappies and insane
My mum she bought the towels in
she didn't make a fuss
she told me about men
and she said 'It's them and us'
mini regular

Super SUPER PLUS
I stuck em on I stuck em in
and then I stuck em up

Stick em on stick em in stick em up gals
stick em on stick em in stick em up
if you wanna sate your lust
then insert a Super Plus
stick em on stick em in stick em up

Remember waiting in the queue
to pay for that first pack
you're looking at the ceiling
with your hands behind your back
then it's you and the assistant
who's since got the sack
says 'DOCTOR WHITE'S MINI PRESS-ON
TOWELS
how much are they Jack?'
Or you're sitting on the toilet seat
one hand between your thighs
the other with instructions
on how to DIY
you hop skip and jump about
you ought to win a prize
and your entire extended family
are queuing up outside

Stick em on stick em in stick em up gals
stick em on stick em in stick em up
if you're paranoid in public
I can't find a better subject
stick em on stick em in stick em up

They have adverts on the telly
to say they are discreet
disposable collapsible
invisible and neat

the ones that make you sit as if
you're one of the elite
and ones that give you ATTITUDE
when walking down the street
The ones that won't go down the loo
however much you try
that bloated towel or tampon
that simply will not die
and some that leak and some you like
and they're the ones you buy
if you're cool rosé is quite passé
you stick to extra-dry

Stick em on stick em in stick em up gals
stick em on stick em in stick em up
if you're thinking of your image
then forget about your spillage
stick em on stick em in stick em up

Well some call it PMS
and some call it PMT
some say it's a deficiency
of vitamin B
some say it is a myth
some say it is reality
but those of us who have it know
it's better post- than pre-
some call it The Curse
from the story of Creation
the Time of the Month
or just menstruation
for the past, the present
and the future generation
I think it's time we gave ourselves
a STANDING OVULATION

Stick em on stick em in stick em up gals
stick em on stick em in stick em up

if you're paranoid in public
I can't find a better subject
stick em on stick em in stick em up

THE EARTH MOTHER

Once upon a time
there lived a wise old woman and a young girl,
one at the beginning, the other at the end
of ripeness but Old Woman craved another child
to chop the wood and mend the roof, a boy
whose skin would sing the tone of potent dark.

She waited for the forest to bleed dark
then ordered Girl to gather lavender, wild thyme,
frogs' legs, a snail's antennae and the special Boy
ingredient: the skinned tail of an Alsatian pup. Girl
set off but being a short-sighted child,
mistook a glow-worm for a dog's tail end.

That weekend
Old Woman made pottage in her womb-dark
cauldron, and she drank, and was with child.
And autumn came and winter went and springtime
lit the black earth with snowdrops. Girl
conversed with snakes and conquered trees while
Boy

grew thumbs and learnt to suck them both. Soon
Boy
grew restless and Old Woman knew her term must
end.
"Look in the convex mirror of my belly, Girl.
Translate to light that which is dark,"
and Girl replied "It's time!"
The forest heaved and wept. The child

was slow to leave its mother, a king-size child
black as a juniper berry. Old Woman named it Boy
and dreamt earth, wind and fire, better times...
And here the tale would end
if little girls could truly tame the dark
and little boys were really boys, not girls.

Old Woman woke and saw her baby Boy was girl
and being wise, gave praise and raised this girl-child
to chop the wood and mend the roof. By dark
the three would eat hot pottage, Girl and Boy
sat side by side, Old Woman at the end
remembering the time,

that first weekend, when the pot bubbled wild thyme
and a child lit up the dark
bowl of her belly, the girl-child she named Boy.

MICHAEL GROCE

Michael Groce was born on 11 January, 1963 in Lambeth, south London. As a child, he lived in Brixton with his mother, who came from Jamaica, and his three younger sisters. He loved living in Brixton:

> Blue sky, summer's haze
> As I bask in Brixton's sun today
> To the sound of Brixton's sunny laughter
> Brixton, shine your sun my way
> ('I love Brixton... can you not see?')

The family was quite poor and Michael was soon to leave, as he recalls: "I hit the streets at a very young age, when I was about six. At the age of seven, I was arrested for being unruly and sent to a children's home in Sussex, where I stayed till I was fourteen. I missed my mother, but I enjoyed my childhood and loved the countryside. Although I was the only black child in the school, people were quite friendly. However, I didn't start to read and write till I was eleven."

He liked most school subjects, loved Physics and his favourite was Maths: "I was not into English, though I liked reading *Huckleberry Finn* and *Tom Sawyer* by Mark Twain. We didn't do any poetry. The school used to do a lot of musicals, like Gilbert and Sullivan's *Pirates of Penzance*, which I really enjoyed and there were plenty of outdoor activities."

Michael believes poetry is often unpopular in school because it is seen as elitist: "My teachers at school made the subjects interesting, but English teachers don't always have the training to make poetry entertaining. I come from a family of entertainers, singers and comedians, so I realise the need to entertain. The poetry also has to be made relevant. Students should see that with a rap artist or song writer, if you take away the music, what have you got left? Poetry. You don't need an English degree to express yourself in a poetic form."

He first came to writing when he was put in prison at an early age: "I used to sit in the cell and I realised I could write love letters really quickly. So I started writing for other boys in the prison. My mother got shot and paralysed by the police and I was very angry for years. I was taking drugs and I decided I wanted to be a writer. My first poem was called 'Charlie Prayer' about my drug addiction':

> The pain of cocaine
> Runs through my very vein
> It's a slave
> To its master
> Bearing shackled chains
> Shackled to my bottle
> I have no focus
> With my life
> Why should I marry
> When Charlie is my wife?

Michael's first poems were very therapeutic, all about himself and his childhood, and his first performance was as a guest spot on a comedy show in Brixton: "It looked easy. I thought I could do that. I walked out on the stage and it was so emotional. The crowd was right on me. Because it was my home town, people knew me. I almost died on the stage. I thought I'm never going do this again! However, when I came off I got a lot of encouragement. I was given the advice of contacting the Poetry Society where there would be an opportunity to learn your craft." He has since performed at many venues, including the Victoria and Albert Museum, Earl's Court, Notting Hill Carnival and the Fridge in Brixton.

As regards publishing his poems, he says: "At first I was very sceptical. I don't have that skill to publish at the moment. If people say, 'Can I have your work?' I say, yes. It's all about spreading the word. My poetry is not a short-term investment. It's going to be my life. If someone says, 'I love those poems you've done. When's the book coming out?' I say, well I've got a couple of the poems in my bag which you can have. I believe in publishing by word of mouth."

Poems come to him at any time. Sometimes he writes by hand, sometimes on the computer: "I can't force a poem. If you have to force it, then it's not going to work well. I normally don't write well unless I have an emotional crisis. If I'm happy, my work gets weak." One poem, entitled 'Blank Page', is about 'writer's block' and begins:

> I tried writing a poem
> But the words wouldn't come
> I sat and thought
> Sat and tried
> Thought of some pretty verse
> But it sounded like a lie
> So I sat again
> Head in my hands
> Think of a master poem
> Was the master plan
> No poem came
> No rhyming words
> A touching phrase... master verse
> > Just a blank page...

Some of the themes of his poetry are hopes and dreams, oppression and inspiration: "I believe poetry can change lives, it can change attitudes. My main purpose is unity, so we can all come together." He was asked, for example, to do a poem about the Irish struggle: "I realised it was the same struggle as black people's. I thought what's in common between the Irish and black people from the Caribbean: we love Guinness punch; they love a Guinness! So, instead of writing about slavery, I designed the whole concept around Guinness and the result was 'Afro Irish'."

Another poem, called 'Inspire', begins:

> I want to inspire I want to inspire
> Like the phoenix rising up from the fire

> I want to inspire I want to inspire
> Like the phoenix rising up
>
> I want to talk about the downfall
> Of greed and desire
> I want to speak the truth
> Expose every liar
>
> I want to talk about things
> On a more positive note
> Talk to the children
> Offer them hope

Michael's favourite poets are T. S. Eliot, Byron and Benjamin Zephaniah. He has appeared on stage with Benjamin Zephaniah and particularly admires his skill as a performer. He has been influenced and inspired by several poets, including John Agard, John Cooper Clarke, Adisa, James Berry and Maya Angelou. Lemn Sissay influenced him in writing a particular poem called 'Colours' which starts:

> No longer will my pen write the blues
> A rainbow of texture that's what I will use
> For I want to see all the Colours that life has to give
> I want to see it all I want to live

His advice to anyone starting to write poetry is: "Say what you think and feel, not what people tell you to. The more honest you are in your poem, the stronger it becomes. Keep it true. Write what you know. Write your story."

> Do it with your own voice
> Let many tongues speak the same language
> Bring gifts from your culture
> Reap the past - Harvest
> Give to all an insight
> Show what you want seen
> All in the name of harmony
> Add to each other's well-being

Let us experience the experience
Touch us all with your culture's beauty
By bringing us the understanding
So that tomorrow means the word unity
Within the moment of the gesture
Help us all to grow
Share with us all the gift
And let the world know
('Let the world know')

AFRO IRISH

The Irish voices were singing
The Afro beat was drumming
Irish music was playing
Let the Guinness flow

Let the Guinness flow my friend
The black and white together
For the history of our paths
Will be entwined forever
From the Irish seas
To the Celtic shores
To the distant roots of motherland
Is the inspiration for our source

For we seem to tell the same story!
It's the same story we tell our daughters and our
sons
As we recollect and ponder
About all those negative things that's been done

Imagining...

The painful cries of slavery
Smelling the death of freedom wars
As so many of our people
Bravely died for the cause

And as they journeyed across the Atlantic
Many becoming victims of the seas
They will gaze towards their motherlands
As returning home would become a dream

But the Irish voices kept on singing
And the Afro heart kept on thumping
And the Irish music kept on playing
Let the Guinness flow

So let the Guinness flow my friend
The black and white together
For the history of our paths
Will be entwined forever
From the Irish seas
To the Celtic shores
To the distant roots of our motherland
Is the inspiration for our source

For we seem to tell the same story!
It's the same story we tell our daughters and our
sons
As we recollect and ponder
About all the negative things that's been done

And the Irish voices kept on singing
And the Afro heart kept on thumping
And the Irish music kept on playing
And the Afro heart kept on drumming
And both voices kept on singing
And both hands kept on clapping
And together they kept on saying
Let the Guinness flow

Let the Guinness flow

Let it flow

IT ALL HELPS...

Rolling hills
Grass that sways
Anchored ships
To sit beneath the blue sky

Artist draws inspiration
Writer scribe the words
All to fill the canvas
All to build a verse

The seagulls are singing their own lullaby
Flock of birds that migrate
Low tide of the early morning
It all helps to create

Salted air that tingles the nostril
Cool breeze that blows against my face
Walks along the pebbled beaches
It all helps to make me feel complete

No loud noise of the city
No traffic that pollutes the air
No sirens screaming in the background
Which all helps to what I hate

The clouds here tell their own story
The sky now becomes the page
Bordered by the distant tree tops
It all helps to what I appreciate

The rolling hills
Grass that sways
Anchored ships
To sit beneath the blue sky

BRIXTON ROCKS...

West London is full of love
South London has the buzz
Which creates abundant vibes
With sights and sounds to open the mind

All human kind gel and flow
Always on the constant go
The spiritual vibe is guiding the night
The poetic nectar keeping us high

We're in a metropolis -
A melting pot of subliminal jazz
Give me the alternative blues
Give me the soca jam

For Brixton rocks and is in the groove
With a heavy baseline keeping it real

Brixton sets the catwalks ablaze
Brixton sets the dreams alight
Encourages colours into unity
The colours of London - to just be

The hub of south London's hopes rest
The places of colours and life
The brick of life that builds foundation
On which the rest of London seeks inspiration

For Brixton rocks and is in the groove
With a heavy baseline keeping it real

The place of cosmopolitan communication
Not spoilt by the people from the institutions
Brixton draws breath - London looks on
For all colours can be Brixtonian

When the snow falls
The sun shines
The rain washes the street
As dusk draws upon us

And people bid
Their farewells
Ciao, adios
And their goodbyes

Brixton rocks and is in the groove
With a heavy baseline keeping it real

CYNTHIA HAMILTON

Cynthia Hamilton was born on 18 April, 1975, in Hammersmith, London. She grew up in an all-female environment with her mother and sister: "My mother is a very strong character and has been a huge influence. We are both alike in being forthright and speaking our minds. She sometimes writes poetry, too. It was my mum who kept discipline and I had a very strict upbringing. At the age of sixteen I still had a curfew at 6pm!"

At primary school, Cynthia loved poetry. She especially liked poems that rhymed or were humorous, like Allan Ahlberg or Roald Dahl's *Revolting Rhymes*, one of which ends with Little Red Riding Hood shooting the Wolf:

> The small girl smiles. One eyelid flickers.
> She whips a pistol from her knickers.
> She aims it at the creature's head
> And *bang bang bang*, she shoots him dead.

At the age of nine, she decided she wanted to be a writer: "First I wanted to be a novelist, not a poet. But I never had the stamina to write a novel. I would write two chapters and then get bored. I wrote plays, too. English was always my favourite subject and I was particularly interested in language. I stumbled upon poetry quite by accident."

At secondary school, Cynthia did a lot of Shakespeare: "We were forced to read *Macbeth* when I was fourteen, but I didn't really understand it at first. I also found the comedies particularly crass. Eventually, *Hamlet* became my favourite play." For 'A' Level she studied the poetry of John Betjeman, Thomas Hardy and Philip Larkin who wrote:

> What are days for?
> Days are where we live.
> They come, they wake us
> Time and time over.
> They are to be happy in:
> Where can we live but days?
>
> Ah, solving that question
> Brings the priest and the doctor
> In their long coats
> Running over the fields.
> ('Days')

She particularly liked John Betjeman, who became Poet Laureate in 1972, because of the structure of his poems. In her job she often has to drive to Slough, so his poem *Slough* has a special resonance:

> Come, friendly bombs, and fall on Slough
> It isn't fit for humans now,
> There isn't grass to graze a cow
>   Swarm over, Death!

Cynthia believes there is a stigma attached to poetry: "It intimidates people. They assume in advance that they're not going to understand it and they think they're going to be extremely bored by it. Performance poetry sometimes attracts people who are very self-indulgent. I've sat through performances that I think are absolutely dire. They're not actually sharing anything with the audience; instead they're doing something very selfish. The major crime of a performance poet is boring your audience!"

She started writing poetry in her late teens. One, about her sister, was called 'The Moody Jersey Cow', which her sister still likes! Her first performance was at a vegetarian restaurant in Liverpool, where she was at university studying English and Writing. As part of the Dead Good Poets' Society, she performed at a 'slam' in Bristol and won first prize. She has also performed at many other venues, for example in Covent Garden, Swindon and Cheltenham, where she became UK Slam Champion of 1996.

There is a difference, for Cynthia, between poetry on the page and on the stage: "Performance poetry comes alive, as the audience wants entertaining. It is also different from a recital when you just stand at a podium and read from a book. Instead, you throw your whole self into the poem. I always feel there's something lost from my poetry when it's on the page, because I'm not there to give it that extra expression and meaning." She thinks publishing is important too, however, "in order to reach as many people as possible. But there is a prejudice among publishers against performance poetry."

Some of her favourite poets are Clare Pollard (whose book *The Heavy-Petting Zoo* contains poems, most of which were written while she was still at school), John Cooper Clarke, Simon Armitage, John Hegley and the American writer, Dorothy Parker who famously wrote:

> Men seldom make passes
> At girls who wear glasses.

She especially likes Roger McGough for his use of wordplay, as for example in 'Penultimate Poem':

> Pen ultimate
> She said
> So I wrote:
> The End.

Poets who have influenced her include Benjamin Zephaniah and Dorothy Parker for her wit and humour, as in 'Unfortunate Coincidence':

> By the time you swear you're his,
> Shivering and sighing,
> And he vows his passion is
> Infinite, undying –

Lady, make a note of this:
One of you is lying.

Cynthia takes a book and pencil with her everywhere: "I've still got the book with all this writing in it and there's no crossing out. But when I write on the computer, there are plenty of deletions. Sometimes I'm too frightened to write in case I write something terrible. I write when I travel and I used to get really good ideas just when I was about to go to sleep. I once woke my sister by jumping out of bed in the middle of the night to write something down."

She sometimes gets 'writer's block', but says: "The way round it is to force it. Don't wait for inspiration. If you're a writer, then you write, that's what you do. Even if you suspect it might not be good, that's not the point. Poetry is a contrivance and you're supposed to work on it. You have to put your heart and soul into it. The performance itself also sometimes helps, as you find that the word you were looking for suddenly comes to you on the night."

One of the themes of her poetry is violence, though it is often disguised with humour, as in 'Likened To Misery' or 'Raping the Skirt'. Another is food and eating, for example 'Dieter's Revenge' or 'Gluttony' which begins:

Is gluttony a deadly sin
Or is it just a way
To cultivate a double chin
In which to catch your gravy in
And make a foul display?

Her poems are often sad and funny at the same time, like 'Contradictoria'. Sometimes, they have a macabre quality, for instance 'Wouldn't Be Seen Dead in One of Your Coffins':

He's a low-budget undertaker,
Penny-pinching moneymaker,
Likes a person better when they're clinically dead.

He's a gold-digging gravedigger,
Likes to make the figure bigger,

Stores the hymns and extra limbs away, inside the shed.

He's a man without morality
Who profits on mortality,
He'll sell your inner organs to the butcher, I expect.

He's a cold-blooded coffin-creeper,
Underhanded profit-reaper,
If he is your undertaker, try to resurrect.

As well as writing poems, Cynthia also writes screenplays, monologues and plays. She has recently collaborated on a play for Radio 4. One of the characters is Jamaican and in writing the play she acknowledges her debt to Louise Bennett.

Having run the poetry section of a bookshop, she sees the way people value poetry: "People often look for a poem when they feel at their lowest, and vice versa – even those who say they don't like poetry. What people buy most are anthologies, particularly of love poems."

Her ironic advice to poets is: "Find that wrong person today! Inspiration often comes from heartbreak. Poetry often comes from the deepest, darkest places."

CONTRADICTORIA

I love you, I love you, I hate you,
I hate you, I love you, I don't.
I want you – I just want to hate you
I just want to love you, but won't.

You make me unhappy, I hate you,
I loathe you, and that is a fact.
Get out of my life or I'll kill you.
Hey, where are you going? Come back!

Don't leave me, I love you, I loathe you.
You're brutal, you're charming, you're mean.
You're my one and only, I love you.
Get out of my sight or I'll scream!

I love you, you're special, you're nothing.
You're no one, you're someone quite dear.
I hate you, I miss you, I love you.
I hope that I've made myself clear.

LIKENED TO MISERY

She gazed at her husband in the hospital bed,
Opened her mouth and calmly said:
'He suffered quite a bump on the head.
Will he die?'

The doctor present only smiled,
Coughed and sighed, and then replied:
'No one I know has ever died
From such a bump.'

The wife then cried: 'I know, I know,
It's just the severity of the blow...
I hope the scarring doesn't show
For his sake.'

The doctor said in jolly tones:
'Two days and you can take him home.
I think I'll leave you both alone.'
And then he left.

The wife left too, in sudden ardour.
Next time she would hit him harder,
There's a hammer in the larder.
No one will know...

GIN AND PLATONIC

A friendly drink
With friendly friends
That often ends
In drunkenness.

From beer and wine
To lethal blends
Which only bring
Embarrassment.

A whisky sour
Mixed with gin
Can make a friend
Seem glamorous.

And if you tip
Some brandy in
The 'friendly' turns
To amorous.

By break of day
You can't explain
The people lying
Next to you.

Discarded bras
And Haagen Daas
Are usually
An ample clue.

DIETER'S REVENGE

She broke her diet
With fudge cake in favour
Thought she would try it
To monitor flavour
What bad behaviour!
No one could save her
Or turn her away from this path she had chosen

She ate three pizzas (although they were frozen)
The devil was cake and his hooves were all cloven
Fat as a cat on the cream it had stolen
Along with the fish and the steak and the trifle

Apples were gathered and ate by the pie-full
Friends hid the packets and tins just to stifle
This new appetite that shot spite at *Ryvita*

She put on a stone and took up a two-seater
Drank malted milkshakes with cream by the litre
Adding honey made everything sweeter
(Especially when she was making a stew)

Why should she chew
When she found she could ravage
A cake or a pie like a latter-day savage?

The horrors that she could inflict on a cabbage
When served up with Black Forest Pork was
appalling!

Leftovers rarely were left until morning
She couldn't see any purpose in stalling
Or calling a halt to her *quaint little munchies*
That started starvation in five different countries

But something was clear (and she couldn't deny it)

An end wasn't far for this gluttonous riot
She ran out of steam and recovered the quiet
Then padlocked the fridge
And went back to her diet...

RAPING THE SKIRT

The girl upstairs had been attacked
They say that she was badly hurt
We blamed the man,
She'd known him well,
They say the judge had blamed the skirt.

He blamed the skirt which she bought
To wear upon that fateful day,
It showed too much, and was too short,
It clearly made her easy prey.

The judge was mad!
Now that was plain,
He filled me up with acrid loathing,
Let the man get off scot-free,
(I think he jailed the piece of clothing.)

So to men
Who might condemn,
I have a tip that just might work:
If it's the skirt that turns you on
Forget the girl
And rape the skirt.

JAMES BERRY

James Berry was born in 1924 in Boston, in the parish of Portland, north-east Jamaica. The fourth of six children, he was brought up in another coastal village, Fair Prospect. Both places had been former slave plantations. His parents were Church of England and his mother sang in the church choir.

At the age of six and a half, he went to the local school which was a mile and a half away, as he recalls: "After working at home in the mornings, feeding chickens and pigs and looking after the goat, and quickly shoving down a bit of breakfast, I ran to school to try and get in before the bell rang which would cut off all late-comers, who would be caned. I could read quite early, before I was four, and was celebrated in my home. My mother used to bring her friends in to hear me read the Bible. But when I went to school I couldn't write and I remember the teacher holding my hand, which was holding the pencil, and teaching me to write. I was very joyful about this, that when she let it go I could make A."

There was no library in the school or in the neighbourhood: "The nearest one was in Port Antonio, our town, fifteen miles away. I was very frustrated at not having books to read to help me. Any time we had a new reading book in the home, it belonged to everybody in the family and pretty soon the book was always absolutely tattered. We had no Caribbean poetry at school, just English poetry. I was good at composition and writing essays, but had no intention then of writing poetry or stories. We were given 'Memory Gems' - particular selections from poetry books and other character-building statements, to choose one from, to be spoken from memory. The one I chose was:

> I will not waste my spring of youth
> In idle dalliance,
> But will plant rich seeds
> To blossom in my manhood
> And bear fruit when I am old.

"The education was colonial. We were not encouraged to recognise and understand our surroundings. We knew nothing about slavery, other than some dates - nothing about how our ancestors lived and got on. This is something which upset me as I got older. There was nothing to express and inform on our experience and background. We learnt a lot about English kings and queens. We were being drilled and prepared all the time to acknowledge that we were British, while our African/ Caribbean aspects were kept out of sight."

James started writing, when he was eight or nine years old, about religious themes, but says he would "love to have read poems about chickens and birds and goats, mules and pigs, banana and coconut fields, and equally about our hills and the sea". He has made up for that now by writing such poems himself, as can be seen in the following extracts, celebrating childhood:

> Fowls come in ones and groups
> and fly up with a cry
> and settle, in warm air branches.
> Tethered pigs are lounging
> in dugout ground.
> ('Night Comes Too Soon')

> Seeing a woman walking in loose floral frock.
> Seeing a village workman with bag and machete
> under a tree, resting, sweat-washed.
> Seeing a tangled land-piece of banana trees
> with goats in shades cud-chewing.
> ('Childhood Tracks')

> Still a joy to remember
> standing at our palm-fringed beach
> watching sunrise streak the sea.
> Finding a hen's nest in high grass
> full of eggs.
> Galloping a horse barebacked
> over the village pasture.
> ('Bits of Early Days')

In the preface to a recent adult collection of poems, *Hot Earth Cold Earth*, James reflects on his time at school: "Personal discoveries, from when I was young at school, gradually revealed a sense that as a black child I was born into an imprisoned people. I began to see I suffered the lacks of my family. From about eight or nine years old I began to notice how the ex-slave-owners' descendants of my village treated my father automatically as an inferior. And my father accepted his position, as if it was all in the way of things. A terror settled in me that I was placed to grow up in my father's position. Inward, thoughtful, anxious, desperate to read books nobody had, I lived with the dread that lack of money and education and opportunity would condemn me to repeat that same design of life impressed upon my ancestors up to my father. Shelley's line 'I fall upon the thorns of life! I bleed!' could describe the silent state of mind in a continuing pain that gathered itself and became 'Letter to Mother Africa'."

> I sit
> under the mango tree in our yard.
> A woman passes along the village road,
> loaded like a donkey.
>   I remember
> I start my seventeenth year today
> full of myself, but worried, and sad
> remembering, you sold my ancestors
> labelled, *not for human rights*,
> And, O, your non-rights terms were
> the fire of hell that stuck.
> ('In Our Year 1941 My Letter to You Mother Africa')

In 'A Schooled Fatherhood', he remembers again how his father was treated:

> There in my small-boy years that day
> Couldn't believe the shock,
> the blow that undid me, seeing him abused,
> reduced, suddenly. Helpless, without honour
> without respect, he stood indistinct,
> called 'boy' by the white child
> in the parents' look-away, 'don't-care' faces.
> Lost, in a peculiar smile - being
> an error, a denial of the man I copied,
> that big-big man I'm one day to be - he made
> a black history I didn't know swamp me,
> hurt me, terror-hands of a dreaded ghost.

After doing farm work in America during the Second World War, James Berry came to England in 1948 on the *S S Orbita*, three months after the *Empire Windrush*. His first task, after finding a job and somewhere to live in Brixton, was to improve his English. He went to evening school, took correspondence courses and attended the City Literary Institute writing workshops.

He recommends that aspiring poets should go to poetry workshops: "It is very difficult to develop writing poetry well on your own, without someone criticising your work. You want to hear the worst things someone else will say about your poems. You need to have one or two admired people, whose ways of thinking you trust, to tell you your weak and strong points as well. Workshops are most important to help you develop standards you value."

After three years as a dental mechanic's assistant, James worked for 26 years as an international telegraphist with Post Office Cable and Wireless (now British Telecom). Then, in 1977, he took early retirement and began to write full-time, working as writer-in-residence in a Lambeth comprehensive school. He has continued to write stories and poetry, spending time visiting schools, performing his poetry and running writers' workshops. "People are often frightened of poetry. Many teachers are still wary of having to teach it, because it's too difficult and is supposed to be highbrow. When you walk into a classroom you soon recognise when a teacher likes poetry and will enthuse the pupils about it."

He is particularly keen on multicultural education and writes in the introduction to his collection of poems, *When I Dance*: "As a boy growing up in the Caribbean I responded to British white people as if all were English. It is since living in England I've come to recognise and enjoy the musically different and distinct speaking voices of the Irish, Welsh and Scots. In a similar kind of way, some 'best educated' people still talk to me, and respond to me, a black man, as if I've just landed from Mars; thank goodness, that response to me has got less and less."

He goes on to comment on our 'monocultural' past: "In the past, too few poems were crowned sovereign over all other cultures, experiences and voices. Too few poems were selectively celebrated. We've come to a time of change. Again, thank goodness, more and more education reflects change in some meaningful directions. More and more an unexpected school includes material from black people's culture and experience."

One of the main themes of James's poetry is his family. He is also obsessed with his background and ancestral experiences, particularly the "slave plantations where people were so trampled. They worked for generations receiving no pay-packets and having no inheritance to pass on to oncoming generations". Recollecting on himself, he writes:

> I remember
> I am third generation since slavery,
> born into people stricken in traps,
> Eight generations departed
> with a last sigh, aware they leave
> offsprings all heirs to losses,
> to nothing, to a shame, and to faces
> who meet enmity in the offices
> of their land and the world.
> ('In Our Year 1941 My Letter to You Mother Africa')

James writes a lot of poems for children and says: "I'll never be able to write about all the ideas I would like to write about." He has certain expectations of an idea, when writing a poem, so he knows when it is not finished: "You just have to put it down for a while till the rest of it comes. So you have a lot of poems you're working on at the same time. It doesn't all come in one rush."

He compares performance poetry with jazz: "It has the same sorrow - pain, pathos, joy and pure entertainment - which has come out of our experience and our African background - all mixed with British culture and the English language. The 'people's language' was first opened up by Louise Bennett. She dared to speak Creole - as the majority of people spoke - on the radio in the 1940s, and absolutely shocked the whole island. She shook us all into a new awareness of our Caribbean consciousness. This later led to a new status given to the Jamaican language as Nation Language.

"We need the truths of our Creole language form," he says. "It reflects the depths of our past. It speaks and highlights that particular pathway of our historical experience, more thoroughly than standard English alone could do. This does not mean I am saying that standard English should be brushed aside or its use be minimised; it is too much a relevant part of our history and experience. Besides, I myself do find great pleasure and joy in the use of these two inherited language forms."

Some of his favourite poets are Linton Kwesi Johnson, Derek Walcott and Ted Hughes, whom he likes very much for his "kind of regional voice, strong and clear". He admires Shakespeare's wisdom and use of language and sees the Old Testament of the Bible as a source of poetry. He also likes to read poetry from other cultures, in translation, and feel the difference in experience. James's own writing keeps moving on.

TRICK A DUPPY

If you wahn trick a duppy
and wahn walk on *happy happy*
in a moonshine - bright moonshine -
hear how and how things work out fine.

You see duppy. No whisper. No shout.
Make not the least sound from you mouth.
One after the other *straight straight*,
strike three matchsticks alight.
Drop one then two of the sticks ablaze
and before you walk a steady pace
flash dead last match like you drop it
when *smart smart* it slipped in you pocket
to have duppy haunted in a spell
and why so you cannot tell.

But duppy *search search* for third match stick
to vanish only when 6 a.m. come tick.

BOOLOOLOOPS

Is you who have a name impressing my tongue over
a million times going on
who surround me with things and hosannas
and a drive for noon
is you is you
boolooloops is you

Is you who get netted in my spoilt days what
stay ready before we come
and who wrap up with my entanglements
who is my steady eye in drought in hurricane in
snow
is my calm on my flickering flame
who try to wake my hidden eye
who try to give my battered boat some oceaning
is you is you
boolooloops is you

Is you who run away and walk back
who lay down the law and break it up
my dazzler who sun paint with long kiss
my source who earth give her cloak to wear
who saying nothing receive my stealth
with your taste of sea salt
is you is you
boolooloops is you

Is you who know I work for waste
but say I know I walk for abundance
is you I want to know my worst sorrow is
the weight of nothing I give to you
is you I want to know though I meet lame horses
and roads impassable hopes are high
is you I want to know often I dress you with hibiscus
and startle you with your worth in delicate lights
is you I want to know my desperate passion not

desolate
not always a solitary cry
is you is you I want to know
boolooloops is you

LISTEN BIG BRODDA DREAD, NA!

My sista is younga than me.
My sista outsmart five-foot three.
My sista is own car repairer
and you nah catch me doin judo with her.

I sey I wohn get a complex.
I wohn get a complex.
Then I see the muscles my sista flex.

My sista is tops at disco dance.
My sista is well into self-reliance.
My sista plays guitar and drums
and wahn see her knock back double rums.

I sey I wohn get a complex.
I wohn get a complex.
Then I see the muscles my sista flex.

My sista doesn mind smears of grease and dirt.
My sista'll reduce yu with sheer muscle hurt.
My sista says no guy goin keep her phone-bound -
with own car mi sista is a wheel-hound.

I sey I wohn get a complex.
I wohn get a complex.
Then I see the muscles my sista flex.

IN-A BRIXTAN MARKIT

I walk in-a Brixtan markit,
believin I a respectable man,
you know. An wha happn?

Policeman come straight up
an search mi bag!
Man - straight to me.
Like them did a-wait fi me.
Come search mi bag, man.

Fi mi bag!
An wha them si in deh?
Two piece of yam, a dasheen,
a han a banana, a piece a pork
an mi lates Bob Marley.

Man all a suddn I feel
mi head nah fi me. This yah now
is when man kill somody, nah!

'Tony,' I sey, 'hol on. Hol on.
Tony. Dohn shove. Dohn shove.
Dohn move neidda fis, tongue
nor emotion. Battn down, Tony.
Battn down.' An, man, Tony win.

JEAN 'BINTA' BREEZE

Jean 'Binta' Breeze was born on the 11 March, 1956, in Patty Hill, in the parish of Hanover, western Jamaica.

She recalls her early interest in poetry: "I did lots of poetry from very, very young, mostly from my mother. She knew lots of poems and she taught them all to me."

An old man going a lone highway
Came at the evening cold and gray
To a chasm vast and deep and wide
Through which was flowing a swollen tide.
The old man passed to the other side.

From the age of five or six, Jean was always being asked to recite poems, either for church or for school concerts, so she always saw poetry as performance: "I enjoyed poetry because I met it first without the page." She remembers when she was twelve years old having to learn Rudyard Kipling's 'If' for a church concert.

She started writing when she was about eleven and this is her first poem, which was published in the school magazine:

I must write.
There is no other way
To cure this feeling in me,
This indescribable feeling
That leaves me aching

> To express my thoughts
> I yearn to tell to others,
> Yet I can't
> And so I write.

Most of her poems came out very clearly, without much need for editing and all her early poems tended to have a moral: "One was called 'Post-mortem', which seems deadly serious for an eleven-year-old!"

Jean had a wonderful time at school: "I always enjoyed school. I liked all subjects at high school, but my favourite was Geography. Poetry was also very enjoyable. I studied T. S. Eliot, for example, at 'A' Level, and I have loved his poems ever since. Whether people enjoy poetry at school is kind of pot luck – it's a matter of which poets are chosen for the courses and whether there is anything in your own experience that makes it fit. I had really good teachers who really loved the poetry. Most of my teachers were expatriates from England. For example, I had a graduate from Oxford teaching me for my 'O' and 'A' Levels, called Giles Wilkinson, and he was very enthusiastic. I had to study Wordsworth:

> I wandered lonely as a cloud
> That floats on high o'er vales and hills,
> When all at once I saw a crowd,
> A host, of golden daffodils.

"I had never seen a 'golden daffodil', but I still liked the poem!"

A lot depends on the teachers: "Sometimes teachers are not confident about voicing poetry and I think poetry needs to be voiced. It's harder to just come at it from a book. If you meet someone who teaches you, who has a good voice and a gift for reading poetry, it makes a big difference to how you hear it."

After she left school she started writing political poems, particularly about the land question in Jamaica: "From about 1976, I used to read at a lot of youth political rallies round the country, at the time when Michael Manley was re-elected as prime minister. There were a lot of changes in land policy in Jamaica and many of the idle plantations were taken over and made into communal farms. So I was used to performing to very large audiences."

In 1983, she and a friend published her first book of poems in Jamaica. It was called *Answers* – "a very embarrassing book!" Then, in 1988, *Riddym Ravings* was published in England by Race Today. Her most recent collection of poems is called *The Arrival of Brighteye,* after the title of one of the poems, which is about a little girl leaving Jamaica to come to England and join her mother:

> My mommy gone over de ocean
> My mommy gone over de sea
> she gawn dere to work for some money
> an den she gawn sen back for me

Since coming to England, Jean has performed her poetry all over the world, from Africa to Asia to America: "I've always had very good responses. I think that's to do with the fact that I'm trained as an actress and the stage is a very comfortable place for me. I found in Asia they were very interested in politics. I remember a young Indian boy in Singapore bringing me a Mandela tee-shirt."

She writes wherever she happens to be when the inspiration for the poem comes, "whether I'm on a train, whether it's on the back of a cigarette packet, whether I happen to be at the computer, whether it's in the middle of the night and I get up and jot it in a note-book. I wrote 'Riddym Ravings (the Mad Woman's Poem)' at four o'clock in the morning. I just got up out of my sleep and went downstairs and wrote it. And then went back to bed!"

Mervyn Morris has called this poem "one of the greatest performance poems in Caribbean literature".

Jean has 'writer's block', as she says, almost permanently. "I'm not a very prolific writer. I don't worry when I'm not writing. There are plenty of other things to be doing. I do a bit of acting. I write films sometimes. I'm a mother of three children, so I spend a lot of time when I'm home in the Caribbean just mothering the children. My son is now twenty-four and plays professional cricket in England."

Her favourite poet is T. S. Eliot "for his music and wonderful sense of conversation and the fact that he is really easy to perform". Her favourite poem is Eliot's 'The Love Song of J. Alfred Prufrock' which ends:

We have lingered in the chambers of the sea
By sea-girls wreathed with seaweed red and brown
Till human voices wake us, and we drown.

She has met other poets who have influenced her: "Mervyn Morris, the Jamaican poet, taught me a lot about editing my work; and Kamau Brathwaite, from Barbados, was very special to me. When I first heard him speak in 1978, I was amazed. It was like he pointed me all the way back home to the village where I was born and I had a strong sense of where I was coming from because of what he said. I like his poetry very much." One of his poems, 'Horse Weebles', begins:

Sellin biscuit an salfish in de plantation shop at pie corner, was another good way of keepin she body an soul-seam together

she got she plot of cane, she cow, she fifteen pigeons in a coop,
razzle-neck fool-hens, a rhode islan' cocklin,
yam, pumpkin, okro, sweet
potato, green pea bush

Jean recognises that there is a recurring theme in her poetry: "I'm always writing women's voices – women's voices from the Caribbean and from Black Britain."

de simple tings of life, mi dear
de simple tings of life

she rocked the rhythms in her chair
brushed a hand across her hair
miles of travel in her stare

de simple tings of life

ah hoe mi corn
an de backache gone
plant mi peas

arthritis ease

de simple tings of life

leaning back
she wiped an eye
read the rain signs
in the sky
evening's ashes
in a fireside

de simple tings of life
('simple tings' - for Miss Adlyn and Aunt Vida)

In 'The Wife of Bath speaks in Brixton Market' she draws inspiration
from Chaucer's *Canterbury Tales* and the Bible:

My life is my own bible
wen it come to all de woes
in married life
fah since I reach twelve,
Tanks to Eternal Gawd,
is five husban I have
                (if dat is passible)
but all of dem was wort someting
in dem own way
doah dem say
dat troo Jesas only go to one weddin
in Canaan
we no suppose fi married
more dan once
but den again
dem say Im tell de Samaritan woman
by de well
dat doah she did have five husban
de laas one never count
        is wat Im mean by dat
        why jus de fif one lef out

ow much she can have den
          four?

Her advice to young poets is: "Live! If you don't have anything to say, why are you going to write? What makes you want to say anything? It's your life, your life experiences. So, you can't play safe with life and expect to have interesting things to say."

ORDINARY MAWNING

it wasn't dat de day did start out bad
or dat no early mawning dream
did swing mi foot
aff de wrong side of de bed

it wasn't dat de cold floor
mek mi sneeze
an mi nose run wid misery
wasn't a hangover headache
mawning
or a worry rising mawning

de sun did a shine same way
an a cool breeze
jus a brush een aff de sea
and de mawning news
was jus de same as ever
two shot dead
truck lick one
Israel
still a bruk up
Palestine
and South Africa still have de whole world han
twist back a dem

no
it wasn't de day dat start out bad
wasn't even pre m t
or post m t
was jus anadda ordinary get up
get de children ready fi school
mawning
anadda what to cook fah dinna dis evening
mawning
anadda wish me never did breed but Lawd
mi love dem mawning

jus anadda wanda if ah should a
tek up back wid dis man it would a
ease de situation mawning

no
it wasn't no duppy frighten mi
mek mi jump outa mi sleep
eena bad mood
nor no neighbour bring first quarrel
to mi door
wasn't de price rise pon bus fare
an milk an sugar

was jus anadda
same way mawning
anadda clean up de mess
after dem lef mawning
a perfectly ordinary
mawning of a perfectly
ordinary day
trying to see a way
out

so it did hard fi understand
why de ordinary sight of
mi own frock
heng up pon line
wid some clothespin
should a stop mi from do nutten
but jus
bawl

RIDDYM RAVINGS
(THE MAD WOMAN'S POEM)

de fus time dem kar me go to Bellevue
was fi di dactar an de lanlord operate
an tek de radio outa mi head
troo dem seize de bed
weh did a gi mi cancer
an mek mi talk to nobady
ah di same night wen dem trow mi out fi no pay de rent
mi haffi sleep outa door wid de Channel One riddym
      box
an de DJ fly up eena mi head
mi hear im a play seh

Eh, Eh,
no feel no way
town is a place dat ah really kean stay
dem kudda - ribbit mi han
eh - ribbit mi toe
mi waan go a country go look mango

fah wen hungry mek King St pavement
bubble and dally in front a mi yeye
an mi foot start wanda falla fly
to de garbage pan eena de chinaman backlat
dem nearly chap aff mi han eena butcha shap
fi de piece a ratten poke
ah de same time de mawga gal in front a mi
drap de laas piece a ripe banana
an mi - ben dung - pick i up - an nyam i
a dat time dem grab mi an kar mi back a Bellevue
dis time de dactar an de lanlord operate
an tek de radio plug outa mi head
den sen mi out, seh mi alright
but - as ah ketch back outa street
ah push een back de plug
an ah hear mi DJ still a play, seh

Eh, Eh,
no feel no way
town is a place dat ah really kean stay
dem kudda - ribbit mi han
eh - ribbit mi toe
mi waan go a country go look mango

Ha Haah... Haa

wen mi fus come a town
mi use to tell everybady 'mawnin'
but as de likkle rosiness gawn outa mi face
nobady nah ansa mi
silence tun rags roun mi bady
in de mids a all de dead people dem
a bawl bout de caast of livin
an a ongle one ting tap mi fram go stark raving mad
a wen mi siddung eena Parade
a tear up newspaper fi talk to
sometime dem roll up
an tun eena one a Uncle But sweet saaf
yellow heart breadfruit
wid a piece a roas saalfish side a i
an if likkle rain jus fall
mi get cocanat rundung fi eat i wid
same place side a weh de country bus dem pull out
an sometime mi a try board de bus
and de canductar bwoy a halla out seh
'dutty gal, kum affa de bus'
ah troo im no hear de riddym eena mi head
same as de tape weh de bus driva a play, seh

Eh, Eh,
no feel no way
town is a place dat ah really kean stay
dem kudda - ribbit mi han
eh - ribbit mi toe
mi waan go a country go look mango

so country bus, ah beg yuh
tek mi home
to de place, where I belang

an di dutty bway jus run mi aff

Well, dis mawnin, mi start out pon Spanish Town Road
fah mi deh go walk go home a country
fah my granny use to tell mi how she walk fram wes
come a town
come sell food
an mi waan ketch home befo dem put de price pon i
but mi kean go home dutty?
Fah mi parents dem did sen mi out clean
Ah!
See wan stanpipe deh!
So mi strip aff all de crocus bag dem
an scrub unda mi armpit
fah mi hear de two mawga gal dem laas nite
a laugh an seh
who kudda breed smaddy like me?
A troo dem no know seh a pure nice man
weh drive car an have gun
visit my piazza all dem four o'clock a mawnin
no de likkle dutty bwoy dem weh mi see dem a go
        home wid
but as mi feel de clear water pon mi bady
no grab dem grab mi
an is back eena Bellevue dem kar mi
seh mi mad an a bade naked a street
well dis time de dactar and de lanlord operate
an dem tek de whole radio fram outa mi head
but wen dem tink seh mi unda chloroform
dem put i dung careless
an wen dem gawn
mi tek de radio
an mi push i up eena mi belly
fi keep de baby company

fah even if mi nuh mek i
me waan my baby know dis yah riddym yah
fram before she bawn
hear de DJ a play, seh

Eh, Eh,
no feel no way
town is a place dat ah really kean stay
dem kudda - ribbit mi han
eh - ribbit mi toe
mi waan go a country go look mango

an same time
de dactar and de lanlord
trigger de electric shack
an mi hear de DJ vice bawl out, seh

Murther
Pull up Missa Operator!

BIBLIOGRAPHY

Poetry

Adisa, Opal Palmer (1992) *Tamarind and Mango Women*, Toronto: Sister Vision

Agard, John (1997) *From the Devil's Pulpit*, Newcastle upon Tyne: Bloodaxe

—— (ed.) (2000) *Hello New!*, London: Orchard Books

—— & Nichols, Grace (1994) *A Caribbean Dozen: Poems from Caribbean Poets*, London: Walker Books

Agbabi, Patience (1995) *R.A.W.*, London: Gecko Press

—— (2000) *Transformatrix*, Edinburgh: Payback Press

Ahmad, Rukhsana (ed.) (1991) *We Sinful Women: Contemporary Urdu Feminist Poetry*, London: The Women's Press

Ali, Arif & Hogben, Catherine (1988) *Grass Roots in Verse*, London: Hansib Publications

Angelou, Maya (1994) *The Complete Collected Poems*, London: Virago Press

Anim-Addo, Joan (1998) *Haunted by History*, London: Mango Publishing

Beasley, Paul (ed.) (1994) *Hearsay: Performance Poems Plus*, London: Bodley Head

Bennett, Louise (1966) *Jamaica Labrish*, Kingston: Sangster's

Berry, James (1979) *Fractured Circles*, London: New Beacon Books

—— (ed.) (1981) *Bluefoot Traveller: Poetry by Westindians in Britain*, London: Harrap

—— (1982) *Lucy's Letters and Loving*, London: New Beacon Books

—— (ed.) (1984) *News for Babylon*, London: Chatto & Windus

—— (1985) *Chain of Days*, Oxford: Oxford University Press

—— (1988) *When I Dance*, London: Hamish Hamilton

—— (1995) *Hot Earth Cold Earth*, Newcastle upon Tyne: Bloodaxe

—— (ed.) (1995) *Classic Poems to Read Aloud*, London: Kingfisher

—— (1996) *Playing a Dazzler*, London: Hamish Hamilton

—— (ed.) (2001) *Around the World in Eighty Poems*, London: Macmillan

—— (2002) *A Nest Full of Stars*, London: Macmillan

Black Womantalk (1987) *Black Women Talk Poetry*, London: Black Womantalk

Bloom, Valerie (1983) *Touch Mi; Tell Mi*, London: Bogle-L'Ouverture

—— (1992) *Duppy Jamboree and Other Jamaican Poems*, Cambridge: Cambridge University Press

—— (1997) *Fruits: A Caribbean Counting Poem*, London: Macmillan

—— (1999) *Ackee, Breadfruit, Callaloo*, London: Macmillan

—— (2000) *Let Me Touch the Sky*, London: Macmillan

—— (2000) *The World is Sweet*, London: Bloomsbury

—— (2000) *New Baby*, London: Macmillan

—— (ed.) (2001) *On a Camel to the Moon*, London: Belitha Press

Brathwaite, Kamau (1992) *Middle Passages*, Newcastle upon Tyne: Bloodaxe

Breeze, Jean 'Binta' (1988) *Riddym Ravings*, London: Race Today

—— (1992) *Spring Cleaning*, London: Virago

—— (1997) *On the Edge of an Island*, Newcastle upon Tyne: Bloodaxe

—— (2000) *The Arrival of Brighteye*, Newcastle upon Tyne: Bloodaxe

Brown, Stewart (ed.) (1984) *Caribbean Poetry Now*, London: Hodder and Stoughton

—— (1999) *Elsewhere*, Leeds: Peepal Tree

—— Morris, Mervyn & Rohlehr, Gordon (eds.) (1989) *Voiceprint: An anthology of oral and related poetry from the Caribbean*, Harlow, Essex: Longman

Burnett, Paula (ed.) (1986) *The Penguin Book of Caribbean Verse in English*, London: Penguin

Chatterjee, Debjani et al (1991) *The Sun Rises in the North*, Huddersfield: Smith/Doorstop Books

Collins, Merle (1992) *Rotten Pomerack*, London: Virago

Dabydeen, David (1984) *Slave Song*, Sydney: Dangaroo Press

—— (1988) *Coolie Odyssey*, London: Hansib

D'Aguiar, Fred (1988) *Black British Poetry* in Allnutt, Gillian et al (ed.) *The New British Poetry 1968-88*, London: Paladin
—— (1993) *British Subjects*, Newcastle upon Tyne: Bloodaxe
Dawes, Kwame (1997) *Shook Foil: A Collection of Reggae Poems*, Leeds: Peepal Tree
—— (ed.) (1998) *Wheel and Come Again: An Anthology of Reggae Poetry*, Leeds: Peepal Tree
Evaristo, Bernardine (1994) *Island of Abraham*, Leeds: Peepal Tree
Feinberg, Barry (ed.) (1974) *Poets to the People: South African Freedom Poems*, London: George Allen & Unwin
Figueroa, John (ed.) (1966) *Caribbean Voices: An Anthology of West Indian Poetry Volume 1 Dreams and Visions*, London: Evans Brothers
—— (ed.) (1970) *Volume 2 The Blue Horizons*, London: Evans Brothers
Finnegan, Ruth (ed.) (1978) *The Penguin Book of Oral Poetry*, London: Allen Lane
Goodison, Lorna (1986) *I Am Becoming My Mother*, London: New Beacon Books
—— (1988) *Heartease*, London: New Beacon Books
—— (2000) *Guinea Woman*, Manchester: Carcanet
Grell, Jane (1994) *Doctor Knickerbocker & Other Poems*, Stroud, Gloucestershire: Hawthorn Press
Harper, Michael S. & Walton, Anthony (ed.) (2000) *African American Poetry*, New York: Vintage Books
Hendricks, A. L. (1988) *To Speak Simply*, Sutton: Hippopotamus Press
Hollo, Anselm (ed.) (1964) *Negro Verse*, London: Vista Books
Hughes, Langston (1995) *The Collected Poems of Langston Hughes*, New York: Vintage
Johnson, Linton Kwesi (1974) *Voices of the Living and the Dead*, London: Race Today
—— (1975) *Dread Beat An' Blood*, London: Bogle-L'Ouverture
—— (1980) *Inglan Is a Bitch*, London: Race Today
—— (1991) *Tings an Times*, Newcastle upon Tyne: Bloodaxe
Kay, Jackie (1991) *The Adoption Papers*, Newcastle upon Tyne: Bloodaxe
—— (1998) *Off Colour*, Newcastle upon Tyne: Bloodaxe
Lyons, John (1989) *Lure of the Cascadura*, London: Bogle-L'Ouverture
—— (with Chatterjee, Martin and Sissay) (1991) *The Sun Rises in the North*, Huddersfield: Smith/Doorstop Books
—— (1994) *Behind the Carnival*, Huddersfield: Smith/Doorstop Books

McCarthy (ed.) (1998) *bittersweet: Contemporary Black Women's Poetry*, London: Women's Press

Malik, Abdul (ed.) (1990) *De Homeplace*, London: Panrun Collective

Mapanje, Jack & White, Landeg (1983) *Oral Poetry from Africa: An Anthology*, Harlow: Longman

Markham, E. A. (1989) *Hinterland: Caribbean Poetry from the West Indies & Britain*, Newcastle upon Tyne: Bloodaxe

Mason-John, Valerie (1999) *Brown Girl in the Ring*, London: Get a Grip

Matthews, Marc (1992) *A Season of Sometimes*, Leeds: Peepal Tree

Mordecai, Pamela & Morris, Mervyn (ed.) (1980) *Jamaica Woman: An Anthology of Poems*, Kingston: Heinemann

—— (ed.) (1987) *From Our Yard: Jamaican Poetry Since Independence*, Kingston: Institute of Jamaica Publications

Nichols, Grace (1984) *The Fat Black Woman's Poems*, London: Virago

—— (1989) *Lazy Thoughts of a Lazy Woman*, London: Virago

—— (1996) *Sunris*, London: Virago

Philp, Geoffrey (2001) *Xango Music*, Leeds: Peepal Tree

Pollard, Velma (1992) *Shame trees don't grow here*, Leeds: Peepal Tree

Poyzer, Darren (ed.) (1994) *Excite The Mind*, Edinburgh: AK Press

Ramchand, Kenneth & Gray, Cecil (1984) *West Indian Poetry*, Harlow: Longman

Roach, E. M. (1992) *The Flowering Rock*, Leeds: Peepal Tree

Sanchez, Sonia (1995) *Wounded in the House of a Friend*, Boston: Beacon Press

Senior, Olive (1994) *Gardening in the Tropics*, Toronto: McClelland & Stewart

Sherman, Joan R. (ed.) (1992) *African-American Poetry of the Nineteenth Century: An Anthology*, Urbana and Chicago: University of Illinois Press

Siffre, Labi (1993) *Nigger*, Abergavenny, Gwent: Xavier Books

—— (1995) *Blood on the Page*, Abergavenny, Gwent: Xavier Books

Sissay, Lemn (1988) *Tender fingers in a clenched fist*, London: Bogle-L'Ouverture

—— (1992) *Rebel Without Applause*, Newcastle upon Tyne: Bloodaxe

—— (ed.) (1998) *The Fire People*, Edinburgh: Payback Press

—— (1999) *Morning Breaks in the Elevator*, Edinburgh: Payback Press

Smith, Michael (1986) *It A Come*, London: Race Today

Springer, Eintou Pearl (2000) *Moving Into the Light*, Kingston: Ian

Randle Publishers
Sulter, Maud (1985) *As A Blackwoman*, Hebden Bridge: Urban Fox Press
Tafari, Levi (1987) *Duboetry*, Liverpool: The Windows Project
—— (1989) *Liverpool Experience*, Neustadt: Michael Schwinn
—— (1993) *Rhyme Don't Pay*, West Kirby: Headland Publications
Walcott, Derek (1981) *Selected Poetry*, Oxford: Heinemann
—— (1992) *Collected Poems*, London: Faber and Faber
Zephaniah, Benjamin (1980) *Pen Rhythm*, London: Page One
—— (1985) *The Dread Affair*, London: Arena
—— (1988) *Inna Liverpool*, Liverpool: Africa Arts Collective
—— (1992) *City Psalms*, Newcastle upon Tyne: Bloodaxe
—— (1994) *Talking Turkeys*, London: Viking
—— (1996) *Funky Chickens*, London: Puffin
—— (1996) *Propa Propaganda*, Newcastle upon Tyne: Bloodaxe
—— (1997) *School's Out: Poems Not for School*, Edinburgh: AK Press
—— (2000) *Wicked World!*, London: Puffin
—— (2000) *A Little Book of Vegan Poems*, Edinburgh: AK Press
—— (2001) *Too Black, Too Strong*, Northumberland: Bloodaxe

Reference
Adams, L. Emilie (1991) *Understanding Jamaican Patois*, Jamaica: Kingston Publishers
Alleyne, Mervyn C. (1988) *Roots of Jamaican Culture*, London: Pluto
Allsopp, Richard (1996) *Dictionary of Caribbean English Usage*, New York: Oxford University Press
Andrews, William L. et al (1997) *The Oxford Companion to African American Literature*, New York: Oxford University Press
Asante, Molefi Kete (1991) *The Book of African Names*, Trenton, NJ: Africa World Press
Baker, Houston A. (1990) *Long Black Song: Essays in Black American Literature and Culture*, Charlottesville: The University Press of Virginia
Barrett, Leonard E. (1976) *The Sun and the Drum: African Roots in Jamaican Folk Tradition*, Kingston: Sangster's
Baugh, John (1983) *Black Street Speech*, Austin: University of Texas Press
—— (2000) *Beyond Ebonics*, New York: Oxford University Press
Bennett, Lerone Jr. (1993) *The Shaping of Black America*, London: Penguin
Bennett, Louise (1979) *Anancy and Miss Lou*, Kingston: Sangster's
Bernal, Martin (1991) *Black Athena*, London: Vintage

Bodunde, Charles (2001) *Oral Traditions and Aesthetic Transfer: Creativity and Social Vision in Contemporary Black Poetry*, Bayreuth: Bayreuth University

Bolster, W. Jeffrey (1997) *Black Jacks: African American Seamen in the Age of Sail*, Cambridge, Massachusetts: Harvard University Press

Boyd, Herb (1994) *African History for Beginners*, New York: Writers & Readers

Brathwaite, Edward Kamau (1981) *Folk Culture of the Slaves in Jamaica*, London: New Beacon

—— (1984) *History of the Voice*, London: New Beacon Books

Brown, Duncan (1998) *Voicing the text: South African oral poetry and performance*, Cape Town: Oxford University Press

Brown, Lloyd W. (1984) *West Indian Poetry*, London: Heinemann

Brown, William Wells (1995) *The President's Daughter* (first published in 1853), London: The X Press

Campbell, Mavis C. (1990) *The Maroons of Jamaica 1655-1796*, Trenton, New Jersey: Africa World Press

Cassidy, Frederic G. (1961) *Jamaica Talk*, London: Macmillan

Chamberlin, J. Edward (1993) *Come Back to Me My Language: Poetry and the West Indies*, Urbana and Chicago: University of Illinois Press

Chester, Galina & Jegede, Tunde (1987) *The Silenced Voice: Hidden Music of the Kora*, London: Diabete Kora Arts

Cooper, Carolyn (1993) *Noises in the Blood*, London: Macmillan

Dabydeen, David & Wilson-Tagoe, Nana (1997) *A Reader's Guide to Westindian and Black British Literature*, London: Hansib

Davidson, Basil (1984) *The Story of Africa*, London: Mitchell Beazley

Dawes, Kwame (2001) *Talk Yuh Talk*, Charlottesville: University Press of Virginia

Dennis, Ferdinand & Khan, Naseem (2000) *Voices of the Crossing*, London: Serpent's Tail

Douglass, Frederick (1982) *Narrative of the Life of Frederick Douglass, an American Slave* (first published 1845), London: Penguin

Edward, Paul (ed.) (1996) *Equiano's Travels*, London: Heinemann

Edwards, Adolph (1967) *Marcus Garvey 1887-1940*, London: New Beacon Books

Edwards, Viv & Sienkewicz, Thomas J. (1990) *Oral Cultures Past & Present*, Oxford: Blackwell

Ellison, Ralph (1995) *The Collected Essays of Ralph Ellison*, New

York: Random House
Finnegan, Ruth (1970) *Oral Literature in Africa*, Oxford: Clarendon Press
—— (1992) *Oral Poetry*, Bloomington and Indianapolis: Indian University Press
Floyd, Samuel A. Jr. (1995) *The Power of Black Music*, New York: Oxford University Press
Fryer, Peter (1984) *Staying Power: The History of Black People in Britain*, London: Pluto Press
Gates, Henry Louis Jr. (1988) *The Signifying Monkey: A Theory of African American Literature*, New York: Oxford University Press
Gates, Henry Louis Jr. & McKay, Nellie Y. (1997) *The Norton Anthology of African American Literature*, New York: W. W. Norton
Habekost, Christian (1986) *Dub Poetry*, Neustadt, Germany: Michael Schwinn
—— (1993) *Verbal Riddim: The Politics and Aesthetics of African-Caribbean Dub Poetry*, Amsterdam: Rodopi
Hareven, Tamara K. (1971) *Anonymous Americans*, New Jersey: Prentice-Hall
Harris, Joel Chandler (1997) *Jump Again! More Adventures of Brer Rabbit*, San Diego: Voyager Books
Holloway, Joseph E. (1991) *Africanisms in American Culture*, Bloomington and Indianapolis: Indiana University Press
hooks, bell (1999) *Remembered Rapture: The Writer at Work*, London: Women's Press
Hoyles, Asher & Martin (1999) *Remember Me: Achievements of Mixed-Race People Past & Present*, London: Hansib
Hurston, Zora Neale (1986) *Their Eyes Were Watching God* (first published in 1937), London: Virago Press
James, C. L. R. (1980) *The Black Jacobins*, London: Allison & Busby
—— (1980) *Spheres of Existence: Selected Writings*, London: Allison & Busby
Jarrett-Macauley, Delia (1998) *The Life of Una Marson 1905-65*, Manchester: Manchester University Press
Jones, Gayl (1991) *Liberating Voices: Oral Tradition in African American Literature*, Cambridge, Massachusetts: Harvard University Press
Kenyon, Olga (1994) *Black Women Novelists*, London: E. Mellen Press
Knappert, Jan (1989) *The A-Z of African Proverbs*, London: Karnak House
Levine, Lawrence W. (1977) *Black Culture and Black Consciousness*,

New York: Oxford University Press
—— (1993) *The Unpredictable Past: Explorations in American Cultural History*, New York: Oxford University Press
Morrison, Toni (1987) *Beloved*, London: Chatto & Windus
Nettleford, Rex (1993) *Inward Stretch Outward Reach*, London: Macmillan
Newland, Courttia & Sesay, Kadija (2000) *IC3: The Penguin Book of New Black Writing in Britain*, London: Hamish Hamilton
Ong, Walter J. (1982) *Orality and Literacy*, London: Methuen
Owosu, Kwesi (2000) *Black British Culture & Society*, London: Routledge
Patten, 'H' & Clementson, John (1999) *Clever Anansi and Boastful Bullfrog*, London: Frances Lincoln
Pollard, Velma (2000) *Dread Talk: The Language of Rastafari*, University of the West Indies: Canoe Press
Rickford, John Russell & Rickford, Russell John (2000) *Spoken Soul*, New York: John Wiley
Salkey, Andrew (1992) *Anancy's Score*, London: Bogle-L'Ouverture
—— (1992) *Anancy, Traveller*, London: Bogle-L'Ouverture
Sherlock, Philip (1966) *West Indian Folk-tales*, Oxford: Oxford University Press
Sidran, Ben (1995) *Black Talk*, Edinburgh: Payback Press
Smitherman, Geneva (1994) *Black Talk*, New York: Houghton Mifflin
Stearns, Marshall W. (1956) *The Story of Jazz*, New York: Oxford University Press
Stewart, Julia (1997) *African Proverbs and Wisdom*, Secaucus, N. J.: Citadel Press
Stuckey, Sterling (1987) *Slave Culture*, New York: Oxford University Press
Sutcliffe, David (1982) *British Black English*, Oxford: Basil Blackwell
—— & Wong, Ansel (1986) *The Language of the Black Experience*, Oxford: Basil Blackwell
Tanna, Laura (1984) *Jamaican Folk Tales and Oral Histories*, Kingston: Institute of Jamaica Publications
Taylor, Patrick (1989) *The Narrative of Liberation: Perspectives on Afro-Caribbean Literature, Popular Culture and Politics*, New York: Cornell University Press
Thiong'o, Nugugi Wa (1986) *Decolonising the Mind: The Politics of*

Language, London: James Currey

Thornton, John (1992) *Africa and Africans in the Making of the Atlantic World, 1400-1680*, Cambridge: Cambridge University Press

Walker, Alice (1984) *In Search of Our Mothers' Gardens*, London: The Women's Press

Walvin, James (1992) *Black Ivory: A History of British Slavery*, London: HarperCollins

—— (2000) *Making the Black Atlantic: Britain and the African Diaspora*, London: Cassell

Wambu, Onyekachi (ed.) (1999) *Empire Windrush: Fifty Years of Writing About Black Britain*, London: Phoenix

Watson, G. Llewellyn (1991) *Jamaican Sayings*, Tallahassee: Florida A & M University Press

Wilkins, Verna (1999) *Benjamin Zephaniah*, Northwood, Middlesex: Tamarind

Wright, Richard (1993) *Black Boy*, London: Picador